John Stott

Pastor, leader and friend

A man who embodied 'the spirit of Lausanne'

CHRIS WRIGHT ET AL

Foreword by Doug Birdsall

THE DIDASKO FILES

This developing series takes its name from the New Testament Greek verb *didasko*, meaning 'I teach'. We trust it will serve the world's Church by helping Christians to grow in their faith.

The idea for the Didasko project came from the International Fellowship of Evangelical Students (IFES), now in over 150 countries, working to proclaim Christ in the world's universities. *www.ifesworld.org* To extend its reach, the series was transferred to The Lausanne Movement, in which IFES plays an active role. *www.lausanne.org*

www.didaskofiles.com

John Stott: Pastor, leader and friend
© 2012 The Lausanne Movement

Published in collaboration with Hendrickson Publishers Marketing, LLC
PO Box 3473, Peabody, Massachusetts 01961-3473

Photograph credits: A P Dowley, Langham Partnership, John Stott. Used with permission.

Designed by Chris Gander

Printed in Singapore by Excel Print Media
ISBN 978-1-59856-997-1

All royalties from this series will be used for publishing endeavours relating to The Lausanne Movement

John Stott

Pastor, leader and friend

A man who embodied 'the spirit of Lausanne'

EDITOR'S NOTE

From the start we knew it would be impossible to contract such a rich and multi-faceted life into a few pages. But we trust this short format, for all its inadequacy, will open up the story of John Stott's life and ministry to many, in a range of languages.

Readers will find a striking constancy throughout these pages, which is a tribute in itself. The seminal influence over decades of works like *Basic Christianity, Your Mind Matters, Issues Facing Christians Today* and *The Cross of Christ* comes through clearly. Repetition of titles of books, and of references to the same events, has been left intact to retain the integrity of each contribution.

A technical note: (i) Rules governing the use of upper/lower case for the noun 'church' have proved less than straightforward in places. We have therefore used lower case throughout. (ii) We have followed the 1984 NIV in using lower case for the word of God, unless the reference is to Christ.

I am grateful to all the contributors for sharing stories, insights, and perspectives. Some speak for continents, others for movements or ministries; each writer also speaks from a sense of personal appreciation.

Julia Cameron
Oxford, November 2011

GLOSSARY OF INITIALS
CBE Commander of the Order of the British Empire
CICCU *Cambridge Inter-Collegiate Christian Union* is made up of Christian Union groups in each of the Cambridge colleges.
ELT *Evangelical Literature Trust* founded by John Stott in 1971 to provide books for the church in the Majority World. It is now called Langham Literature.
GBU *Groupes Bibliques Universitaires*, the name used by IFES movements in the Francophone world.
LICC *London Institute for Contemporary Christianity* seeks to equip Christians with a robust biblical worldview of their professions, and of cultural and political trends.
IFES *International Fellowship of Evangelical Students* serves national student movements (like UCCF) in over 150 nations. New movements are pioneered as the political and religious situation allows.
NIFES *Nigerian Fellowship of Evangelical Students*, one of the largest IFES national movements.
UCCF *Universities and Colleges Christian Fellowship* (founded as the Inter-Varsity Fellowship) serves the student Christian Unions across England, Scotland and Wales. (Ireland was included until 1999, when a separate movement was established.)

CONTENTS

From the 1974 Congress on World Evangelization, a winsome phrase 'the spirit of Lausanne' emerged. No one could be precise about its provenance, whether from Billy Graham (who himself was not sure), or simply as a phrase that was mused on by someone, repeated, liked and then adopted. While no one was quite sure where it came from, its definition was clear. It was a spirit of prayer, study, partnership, hope and humility. Each one of these components was important to John Stott, and characterized the way he lived. Indeed, Uncle John was a man who embodied 'the spirit of Lausanne'.

He often referred to the phrase, and used it as a reference point for The Lausanne Movement as it developed. To borrow Peter Kuzmic's quip from a Lausanne leadership gathering in Budapest in 2007, John Stott 'war ein Lausanner'.

Through these pages, we are pleased to be able to share and extend our memories and stories of John Stott.

it was a spirit of prayer, study, partnership, hope and humility

He loved the work of The Lausanne Movement and gave much of himself to it from the time of the first Congress in 1974. You will read of that on p55. His role as chief architect of *The Lausanne Covenant* is well known. The days of meetings, and his weeks of work in editing the historic documents of the Movement are less well known. *The Lausanne Covenant* gave definition to the Movement and, through it, to contemporary evangelicalism. In the second congress (Lausanne II in Manila, 1989) John Stott served both as a Bible expositor, and as chief architect of *The Manila Manifesto*, a document he considered on a par with *The Lausanne Covenant*.

Shortly after I became Chair of The Lausanne Movement in 2004, I called Uncle John to ask if he would be willing to serve as Honorary Chairman. Happily, he accepted after giving the matter careful and prayerful consideration over the period of a few weeks. Though it was an honorary role, he wanted to be kept informed, and he enjoyed being a part of the discussion of key issues.

It was a particular pleasure to talk about the planning for the Third Lausanne Congress in Cape Town in 2010. Very early in the dreaming process we met for dinner at a restaurant near his London home, to think and talk about the possibility of a third congress. As we walked back to his flat that evening, he held a cane in one hand and held my elbow with the other. He said to me, 'I just hope I live long enough to see this come to reality.' He did live long enough to see the vision for the Third Lausanne Congress come to reality. And, he had the joy of encouraging his friend, Chris Wright, as he chaired the Theology Working Group, and served as the primary architect for *The Cape Town Commitment.*

Ajith Fernando writes of the Lausanne Younger Leaders Conference in Singapore in 1987. I, too, would testify to how the three hundred of us there were profoundly impacted by the way John Stott spent ten days with us, mentoring, encouraging and sharing meals together.

Almost every time we met together, he would enquire about Billy Graham. Actually, we had made plans for Billy Graham and John Stott to meet at the Grahams' home in North Carolina in the autumn of 2006. Both men were eager to have one more visit. Sadly that meeting did not take place as Uncle John had to cancel the trip due to breaking his hip in a fall that would signal the end of his travels.

When I asked him if he would write a letter in support of Cape Town 2010, he enquired, 'Will Billy be writing too?' I told him that Dr Graham had also agreed to write, and he said he would like to see Billy Graham's letter first. 'As the founder of the Movement, Billy should have the first word,' he said. His deference to Billy Graham was an expression of his admiration for him, and another example of humility and graciousness.

when I called, his friend was reading it aloud to him

In April 2011, I called John Stott from Boston to share my delight in receiving my first copy of the recently completed *Cape Town Commitment*. I found that he had received his copy a few days earlier, and when I called, his long time friend Phillip Herbert, was reading it aloud to him. Though John's voice was very weak, his joy was unmistakable. 'You seem to have achieved an astonishing degree of unity,' he said. 'Chris [Wright] and his team did a masterful job!'

for him the concert now 'goes on forever'

My first encounter with John Stott had been at a performance of Handel's *Messiah* in the Edman Chapel at Wheaton College, in Illinois, in my student days. We talked briefly during the intermission and again after the concert at which time he said, 'I wish it could have gone on forever!' When Chris Wright wrote to tell me of John Stott's home going, he said the friends who were with him had played him Handel's *Messiah*, 'I know that my Redeemer liveth.' For him, the concert now goes on forever!

Knowing that John Stott is now with the Lord makes the anticipation of Heaven that much greater. Knowing that our pastor, leader and friend is now among that great cloud of witnesses makes our commitment to run the race with endurance that much stronger.

Revd Dr S Douglas Birdsall *is Executive Chairman of The Lausanne Movement. Doug and his wife spent twenty years in Japan with Asian Access. Since 1999 Doug has served as the Director of the J Christy Wilson Center for World Missions at Gordon Conwell Theological Seminary, Boston.*

JOHN R W STOTT

John Robert Walmsley Stott, fourth child and only son of Sir Arnold Stott, Extra Physician to the Royal Household, and Lady (Lily) Stott, died on the afternoon of 27 July 2011, in the College of St Barnabas, a home for retired clergy, in Surrey, England. He joined the Sunday School at All Souls, Langham Place as a small child, and was to serve its congregation and parish as assistant curate, Rector and Rector Emeritus. His global ministry remained anchored here throughout his life.

John Stott's childhood was spent in Harley Street and his home remained within a few minutes' walk of All Souls (situated between Oxford Circus and Regents Park) for over eighty-five years. He was a Chaplain to the Queen, honoured with the CBE, and named as one of the '100 most influential people in the world' by *TIME* magazine.[1]

He wore privilege lightly. He turned his Rectory into what was nicknamed the 'Wreckage', sharing it with others and welcoming many guests.[2] From 1970-2007 he lived in a modest two-roomed flat, built above the garage behind the Rectory. John Stott advocated the simple lifestyle, and he practised it.

He was an integrated man, with a deep appreciation of the natural world, and a rather British sense of humour, which never left him. From early childhood his father took him on nature walks, teaching him to watch and to listen. At the same time, his nanny was taking him to the Sunday School at All Souls, armed with toy daggers and a gun, to terrify the girls. (He reputedly spent more time outside the classroom than inside.) In his writing retreat at The Hookses, on the Pembrokeshire coast, he kept his binoculars on his desk, which overlooked the bay with its rich birdlife. A copy of Saki's short stories sat on the bookshelves to his right. He would read Saki to his guests, often laughing so much at the stories that he could barely continue to read them![3] The ability to make people laugh was, he remarked, aged almost 87, 'a forgotten charisma'.

The calling, gifting, *métier*, of this unusually-able man was unique. He had no peer and, as Archbishop Peter Jensen said in the thanksgiving service in Sydney Cathedral, we should not look for a successor. At the thanksgiving service in Vancouver, Prof J I Packer paid tribute to 'a fifteen talent man', and so he was.

As a humble disciple of Christ, he would greet the three Persons of the Trinity in turn each morning, seeking genuinely to live as a son of his heavenly Father, as a sinner saved by grace, and in the power of the Holy Spirit, his advocate and counsellor.

In an interview in 2007,[4] he was asked how he would most like to be remembered. He was by this stage speaking slowly, but there was no hesitation in the content of his response. 'As an ordinary Christian who has struggled to understand, expound, relate and apply the word of God,' he said. His huge output, and the grasp of Scripture which lay behind it, was won only through 'daily dogged discipline'.

It became his pattern to rise early to read and pray, and to listen to the BBC World Service news. Listening to God through scripture should not be removed from world events. As we practise 'double-listening', he would say, we can apply the word of God to his world. Having risen early, John Stott would then rest after lunch. What became known around the world as his HHH (horizontal half hour) became his HH (horizontal hour) in later years.

He loved children, and being an uncle, a great uncle, and a godfather. While he considered marriage twice, he resolved not to marry. He also resolved not to pursue an academic career, or to become a bishop. The stories are told well in his biographies (see p71). Each brought its cost, but his ministry required freedom from the responsibilities these callings would place on him.

John Stott worked to be rooted in the eternal gospel and to apply it, for each decade and each context, with intellectual and theological rigour, perceptiveness, cultural sensitivity – and with an eye to the future.

The global influence of this seminal thinker, humble leader, friend to thousands, and author of over 50 books, will unfold as future church history is written.

Editor

TRIBUTE FROM
JOHN STOTT'S SECRETARY

So many tributes from all over the world have been paid to John Stott. I have asked myself what could I say that has not already been said, by way of thanks to God for John's life, and what it has meant to me and so many others? Let me simply express my gratitude for John himself, his godly example, and his faithful preaching through which the light of Christ first dawned on me.

Because I worked alongside him as his secretary for 55 years, perhaps I more than anybody can testify to the fact that, in his case, familiarity, far from breeding contempt, bred the very opposite – a deep respect, and one which inspired belief in God. The more I observed his life and shared it with him, the more I appreciated the genuineness of his faith in Christ, so evident in his consuming passion for the glory of God, and his desire to conform his own life to the will of God. It was an authentic faith that fashioned his life – it gave him a servant heart and a deep compassion for all those in need, one that moved him to keep looking for ways in which he might be of encouragement and support to others, sharing his friendship and his own resources.

To work with John was to watch a hard-working man of great discipline and self-denial, but at the same time to see a life full of grace and warmth. His standards were high and he took trouble over all that he did; nothing was ever slapdash. He was consistent in every way and always kept his word. Although so gifted himself, he never made me feel inferior or unimportant. Instead, he would share and discuss his thoughts and plans with his study assistant and me, listening to our contributions, and eager to ensure consensus between the three of us – the 'happy triumvirate' as he would call us. So I found him easy to please and ever grateful for one's service.

it was an authentic faith that fashioned his life

The Scriptures lay at the heart of all John's teaching and preaching. His ability to interpret them was not simply a matter of the intellect, but of a heart full of love for Christ, and a longing to serve him faithfully, no matter what the cost in human terms. For he believed and submitted himself to the sovereignty of God and the Lordship of Christ in his own life – and he accepted the authority of the Bible as the word of God, regardless of ridicule by some..

Indeed, John taught and practised what he believed, and I thank God for the way he pointed me constantly to Jesus. 'Don't look at me', he would say. 'Look at Jesus and listen to him.' But he also demonstrated the truth of what he was saying by his own example of obedience. This was the powerful magnet that drew people to put their faith in Christ as the Son of God and Saviour of the world. He believed that Christ lived on earth, died on the cross for our salvation, and will come again one day in glory. He believed that death is not the end, and that there will be a new creation in which we may all share, through repentance and faith in Jesus.

thank God that John deeply believed all these truths

Thank God that John deeply believed all these truths, lived in the light of them, and maintained them, right to the very end. John's life was a wonderful example of what it means to be a true Christian - and what a blessing he was to all those who were privileged to know him.

Frances Whitehead *became John Stott's secretary in 1956, and now serves as one of his literary executors. She was awarded a Lambeth MA in 2001.*

Lambeth MA

Lambeth degrees are not honorary, but regarded as earned. The citation on Frances's MA read:

In recognition of her energetic and enthusiastic ministry to God's Church through her dedicated support of Dr John Stott for over 40 years and for her visible Christian witness.

AN 'ABRAHAMIC AND APOSTOLIC' MINISTRY

Chris Wright sets the scene for the founding of Langham Partnership International

'I am a great believer,' John Stott would say, 'in the importance of BBC. Not the British Broadcasting Corporation, nor Bethlehem Bible College, nor even Beautiful British Columbia. But Balanced Biblical Christianity.'

I would like to suggest that the scale and scope of John Stott's ministry within the global church rested on his biblical balance of Old and New Testaments. He was both Abrahamic and apostolic. Let me explain.

John Stott's mission was 'Apostolic' in nature

John would never have claimed the title 'Apostle' for himself. 'There are no apostles in today's church,' he said, 'with the same status or authority as the unique apostles of the Lord Jesus Christ in the New Testament.' But his ministry was apostolic in the sense that it faithfully reflected the passion and priorities of the biblical apostles: evangelism and teaching.

(i) Evangelism

The apostles proclaimed the good news that Jesus of Nazareth was the promised Messiah and Lord, and called people to receive the salvation God had accomplished through his cross and resurrection by repentance, faith and obedience.

John Stott had the heart of an evangelist from his own teenage conversion to his

his ministry reflected the passion and priorities of the apostles

13

final years in the College of St Barnabas. While still at Rugby School he was helping to run evangelistic camps for boys at Iwerne Minster,[5] and giving talks to lead others to the Saviour. About a year before he died, he told me with some excitement of how he had been able to 'explain the way of salvation' to one of his carers – a woman who asked him a question while wheeling him back from lunch in the dining room. The first of John's international travels (1956-57) was to conduct evangelistic missions on university campuses in the USA, and for years his effectiveness as a university evangelist was the main reason for his growing international ministry. His early book (almost but not quite his first) *Basic Christianity* distilled those evangelistic addresses and has led thousands of people to faith in Christ. And his last book, *The Radical Disciple*, written when he could scarcely hold his pen steady, still breathes the truth and the appeal of the apostolic gospel.

(ii) Teaching

The apostles were tireless in teaching their new churches, by visiting them and writing to them, to ground them in their faith and urge them to grow up in maturity in Christ. In this, just as much as in evangelism, they were doing what Jesus told them in 'the great commission', that is, 'teaching them to obey all that I have commanded you'.

John Stott was as passionate and committed to the work of apostolic teaching as to apostolic evangelism.

Like the Apostle Paul, he longed to see Christians and churches growing up to maturity in Christ, and growing into the likeness of

like the Apostle Paul, he longed to see churches growing up to maturity

Christ. He saw and rejoiced in the numerical growth of the church in the Majority World.[6] But he lamented the lack of teaching, discipling and pastoral leadership that left new churches weak and vulnerable, plagued by spiritual extremism and moral laxity, and at the mercy of self-appointed ►

THE LANGHAM LOGIC

If God wants his people to grow to maturity (which he does); if the Church grows through God's word (which it does); if God's word comes to God's people through faithful preaching (which it does); then the logical question to ask is, 'What can we do to raise the standards of biblical preaching?' For then the word of God will feed the people of God, and they will grow to maturity, and thereby to effectiveness in their mission and their ministry.

This rationale remains the driving engine of Langham Partnership International, which John founded. It began as the Langham Trust in 1969. (Characteristically named, not after himself, but the street where All Souls stands.) This trust provided scholarships to help gifted younger evangelicals gain doctorates and be better equipped as teachers of pastors in their own countries. Next came the Evangelical Literature Trust in 1971, recycling John's own book royalties and other donations to provide books for pastors and seminaries, to resource their biblical preaching. And finally in 2001 John and I pioneered some preaching seminars in Latin America, to motivate and train pastors in the skills of biblical expository preaching. These three initiatives now work together as three programmes: Langham Scholars, Langham Literature and Langham Preaching, under the unifying vision, '*To see churches worldwide equipped for mission and growing to maturity in Christ through the ministry of pastors and leaders who believe, teach, and live by, the word of God.*'

* *Langham Scholars* enables men and women from the Majority World to gain doctorates in Bible and theology. Most then teach future generations of pastors in Bible Colleges and seminaries. Partly as the fruit of this work, new high-quality evangelical seminaries now offer doctoral degrees in Majority World countries. Langham alumni, serving on faculties, nurture future Langham scholars.

▷

▷

- *Langham Literature* provides evangelical books to hundreds of thousands of pastors, and hundreds of seminary libraries. This began with mainly western books in English or translation. Now Langham is increasingly helping to foster indigenous evangelical writers, and editors, with the establishing of new publishing houses in Majority World countries. They feed the minds and hearts of their own people in their own languages and resource pastors and preachers for their primary task. The flagship of this shift is the one-volume *Africa Bible Commentary* written entirely by African scholars for African contexts. Its first edition in English was soon followed by editions in French, Portuguese, Swahili and Malagasi, with plans put in place for Amharic and Hausa. Langham Literature is sponsoring comparable volumes in South Asia, Latin America, and the Arabic-speaking world.

- *Langham Preaching* is creating movements for biblical preaching in more than sixty countries. Here we work with church leaders to arrange (i) training seminars, (ii) local preachers' clubs, (iii) the training of local and national facilitators and trainers, (iv) regional conferences, and (v) the provision of books and other preaching resources. Alongside this we are working to raise the standard of the teaching of preaching in seminaries.

All of these ministries are an expression of 'apostolic teaching', whether that teaching happens in a pulpit, in a classroom, or through the pages of a book. They are comparable to the ministries of Apollos (a scholar teacher), Timothy (a preacher and trainer of others) and even Tertius (a trained writer who wrote Paul's letter to the Romans). All teaching which builds the church (theological education in its broadest sense), is part of the great commission, so is by its nature, missional. There is mission beyond evangelism: the mission of teaching and discipling. Every Paul needs an Apollos.

leaders, exploiting the flock with more greed than grace. Like the Apostle John, he longed for Christians and churches to live in love and unity, and saw our chronic dividedness (particularly among some evangelicals) as visible evidence of immaturity.

he longed for Christians and churches to live in love and unity

'The Langham Logic'

'How would you sum up the state of the Church around the world today?' he would often ask, when introducing the work of The Langham Partnership. 'I can do it in three words, *Growth without depth*. There is much evangelistic growth in numbers. But sadly there is also shallowness and immaturity everywhere, and it is not pleasing to God.' From that challenging start he would go on to articulate what he called 'The Langham Logic', based on three biblical convictions (supported with many biblical texts) and a logical conclusion.

- God wants his church to grow up, not just to grow bigger

- God's church grows through God's word

- God's word comes to God's people mainly (not exclusively) through biblical preaching

John Stott's call was 'Abrahamic'

As we gain perspective on John's ministry, we see two ways in which he mirrored Abraham. The first is the most obvious.

a) Blessing the nations

According to Paul, the gospel was announced in advance to Abraham.[7] This good news of God's promise to bless all nations on earth was ultimately fulfilled through Jesus Christ, and the spread of his gospel to all nations. But the role of God's people has always been 'Abrahamic' in the sense of being *instrumental* in God fulfilling that promise.

In that sense, John Stott was truly Abahamic. His whole life, from a very early stage of his pastoral ministry, was spent in reaching out to the nations of the world. His travels in all

he listened respectfully to other cultures

continents were not just some kind of tourism for Jesus (or sanctified bird-watching). His passion was to gain a global understanding of Christian theology and mission, of what it meant to be the worldwide body of Christ. Wherever he went, he did as his father had told him as a small boy in the countryside – he kept his eyes and ears open. He listened respectfully to other cultures, learned from them, and sought to see the richness of the eternal biblical gospel through the eyes, needs and aspirations of others. It could be said that he was a blessing to so many, in every part of the world, because he opened himself up to be blessed by them.

The extent to which John Stott was Abrahamic in 'blessing the nations' can be seen in the number of international evangelical bodies with which he had close association - The Lausanne Movement, World Evangelical Alliance, IFES, Scripture Union,[8] A Rocha, Tearfund...

b) The obedience of faith

John's ministry was Abrahamic not just in its *scope*, but also in its *substance*. 'By faith Abraham...obeyed'.[9] God's promise came with a demand, that he should walk in the way of the Lord by doing righteousness and justice, and teaching his household to do the same.[10] God's people were to bless the nations by living among them in a way that was ethically distinctive at all levels – political, economic, judicial, familial, sexual, *etc*. God's people are to be, as Jesus put it, salt in a corrupt world and light in a dark world. We can perform that function only by being engaged with every area over which Jesus is Lord. (This means *every* area of life on earth, and even the earth itself as God's creation.)

John Stott was as passionate about the engagement and penetration of the gospel in the everyday public arena, as he was about its truth.

He could not separate them. He would have argued that the truth of the gospel had not been grasped until its radical demands, as well as its gracious promises, were being presented and lived out by 'integrated Christians'. His rejection of the disabling

the biblical gospel brings all of life under Christ

falsehood of a 'sacred-secular divide' led to his founding the London Institute for Contemporary Christianity.

John was not interested in 'the irreducible minimum of the gospel'. He wanted to be faithful to the whole biblical gospel in all its glorious richness and in its transforming power, which brings all of life in heaven and earth under the Lordship of Christ.

In this conviction, and in all he did to give it practical expression, John Stott was Abrahamic and apostolic. The global church has been incalculably blessed by him in both respects. We have much yet to learn and to implement.

Revd Dr Christopher J H Wright *is International Director of Langham Partnership International. He is a special advisor to the Lausanne Theology Working Group, which he formerly chaired. In 2010 Chris chaired the Statement Working Group which was responsible for producing* The Cape Town Commitment.

DAILY BIBLE READING

John Stott's 'Abrahamic and apostolic' ministry was fed by what John Bunyan would have termed 'bibline blood'. He worked daily to get the Bible into his bloodstream, so it informed his thinking and his actions. While in his thirties, a friend had introduced him to a method of reading the whole Bible each year. He loved it, and wanted to pass it on to others. Las Newman explains.

When I was a young theological student in Canada, in the late 1970s, I had the privilege of serving as Uncle John's student aide when he conducted a mission at the University of Toronto. On the last day of the mission he asked me if I was acquainted with Robert Murray McCheyne's Bible Reading Plan. I told him I wasn't.

He said, 'My dear Las, this plan will change your knowledge and grasp of the Bible as a whole.' He handed me a copy, and it has helped me on my journey through the Bible ever since. I found out afterwards that Dr Martyn Lloyd-Jones had, in the 1950s, handed a copy to Uncle John in just the same way, and he used it for the rest of his life. It takes readers through the whole Bible each year, and the New Testament and Psalms twice. But it was designed by McCheyne as a helper, not as a master, and can be followed more flexibly.

It has helped me to balance my devotional and theological reading of the Old and New Testaments in a consistent way. As it was commended to me, so I highly commend it to others.[11]

Dr Las G Newman, *former IFES Associate Gen Sec, is President of the Caribbean Graduate School of Theology, and an International Deputy Director of The Lausanne Movement.*

SERVING THE STUDENT WORLD

John Stott spent the war years from 1940 in Cambridge, first at Trinity College, where he gained a double first in modern languages and theology, and then at the Anglican training college, Ridley Hall. Over these years, his life's ministry was being formed.

His father, a major general in the medical corps, felt a sense of embarrassment that John should spend these days in academia, instead of helping the war effort. But John was firm: as a Christian, he believed he had to be a pacifist. In years to come, he saw that his position was not well informed. No-one had helped him understand the Just War theory. Had he engaged with it, he sensed he would have responded differently. It proved costly for him as it caused grief for his family. Throughout his ministry, he always wanted Christian students to be better helped to formulate ethical judgments than he had been.

As we look back, we see God's wonderful hand of providence even in our mistakes. In John's first week, he made friends with a zoologist, Oliver Barclay, two years his senior. They spent much time together in discussion, walking round and round Trinity Great Court, or along the Backs of the colleges, 'trying to solve all the problems of Church and state'. Friendships built in student years can last for life; the friendship between John Stott and Oliver Barclay was one such friendship.

in Cambridge his life's ministry was formed

Both were immersed in the life of the CICCU and both would serve as its lifelong Honorary Vice Presidents. After Oliver Barclay completed his doctorate, he moved to London to take a new position as Assistant General Secretary in the Inter-Varsity Fellowship (now UCCF). Its founding General Secretary was Douglas Johnson. John Stott had great respect for 'DJ', as he was always known, and would refer to him sixty years later as the greatest single influence on UK evangelicalism.

INTER-VARSITY PRESS

Through Oliver Barclay and Douglas Johnson, John Stott met Ronald Inchley, who, as a recent graduate, founded in 1936 what became Inter-Varsity Press (IVP). Ronald Inchley, known as 'RI', nurtured John as a young author. At that time evangelicals were rather derided. This new publishing house, getting started again after the war, was a modest venture. Inchley, who read English at Birmingham, spent much of the war as a quantity surveyor employed by John Laing Construction, building airfields. Here he learned the delicate balance of costing time and materials against outcome, a new idea in an organization more concerned with ministry than management. He set the publishing venture on a sound footing, and had a shrewd eye for new authors. Soon his list was to include the sharpest evangelical thinkers of the day.[12]

From small beginnings, this operation to produce books for students and graduates was to gain wide credibility in the evangelical church globally. Inter-Varsity Press would become John Stott's main publisher. In addition to the 34 titles it published by him, IVP also published the widely-popular *Bible Speaks Today* (BST) series, of which John Stott was founder and New Testament editor. His books would go into sixty languages.[13]

University missions

The All Souls Church Council gave generously of their pastor's time. For a quarter of a century, starting and ending in his Alma Mater (1952, 1977), John Stott led many university missions across the UK, and around the world. He was highly-gifted as a university evangelist.

he was highly-gifted as a university evangelist

He loved to remind students that a clearly-reasoned presentation of

UNIVERSITY MISSIONS 1952-1977

In Britain and Ireland: Aberdeen • Aberystwyth • Cambridge
Durham • Exeter • Leeds • Leicester • Liverpool • London
Loughborough • Manchester • Newcastle • Nottingham
Oxford • Queen's, Belfast • St Andrews • Trinity College, Dublin

Around the world: Cape Town • Ceylon • Ghana • Harvard
Helsinki • Ibadan • Illinois • Lund • Malaya • Manila • Manitoba
McGill • Melbourne • Michigan • Nairobi • Oslo • Sierra Leone
Singapore • Sydney • Rhodesia and Nyasaland • Toronto
Western Ontario • Witwatersrand • Uganda

the gospel acts as a basis or ground for faith. It is not a replacement for the Holy Spirit's working, but a vehicle of the Holy Spirit, a means by which God's objective truth can be made clear.

John brought a rare combination of gifts to campus ministry. He was an evangelist, a teacher, and an able and patient apologist. He would typically proclaim Christian truth in the evenings, by

professions of faith would come gradually

expounding passages from the gospels; then in smaller contexts, often in a faculty or department, he would listen to students' questions, work back with students to the premise of the question, and engage in reasoned dialogue, modelling a robust Christian mind.

Professions of faith would come gradually, some during the mission week, others later, even much later. In his early years as a missioner, he would preach in clerical robes, often in a church building. By 1977 the world was much more secular, and there was no religious form in the meeting. In the West the venues were, by then, almost all neutral territory.

In each place, John would be the servant of the student mission committee. The student leaders knew the context and were Christ's

I would like to introduce myself to you as a committed 'IFES man' – and that for at least four reasons. IFES is (i) **Biblical**, seeking in all things to be submissive to the supreme authority of scripture; (ii) **Indigenous**, encouraging self-governing national movements; (iii) **Evangelistic**, with students winning students for Christ; and (iv) **Holistic**, seeking to lead new converts to maturity in Christ.

So I thank God for IFES.

John Stott *(Video greeting to the IFES World Assembly in 2007, with its new generation of student leaders)*

aroma in it. He much appreciated the IFES policy of student leadership, and was glad to hold himself accountable to the students. This was, for them, always a wonderfully-memorable learning experience, not only during the mission week, but in all its preparation, and in working to ground new believers in the faith.

John would be the servant of the student mission committee

In addition, he was a regular Bible expositor at the Intervarsity (US and Canada) Urbana Missions Conventions. John, a much-loved Urbana speaker, was invited to return once more in 2003, to give the opening address. He was eighty-two years of age. He managed to join us that summer for the IFES World Assembly in the Netherlands, weaving into the programme his usual schedule of private meetings for those who wanted to talk. Sadly in December ill-health impeded him from going to Urbana, and he had to submit his address, meticulously prepared, to be read for him.[14]

I first met John when I was President of the Christian Union at Oxford. We saw each other often over the years, as I joined UCCF staff, and then served as IFES Regional Secretary for Europe. When John heard news of my appointment in 1991 as IFES General Secretary, he must have remembered his own feelings in becoming a very young Rector of All Souls. National movements had, by that stage, been established in 67 countries, some still very fragile; and much pioneering was still to be done.

He wrote me a kind letter, as always bringing together pastoral advice and spiritual encouragement. In it he quoted the words of John Newton: 'Lindsay, I hope you will be a reed in non-essentials and an iron in essentials.'

When we spoke soon afterwards, he called to mind Martin Luther's words when writing on the Apostle Paul, urging me to be 'strong in truth and soft in love'. He was referring to the need to stand firm on key doctrines, and to allow breadth in matters which were not central. Our doctrinal basis includes only the primary truths of the gospel, the

PREACHING TO STUDENTS

I shall never forget the impact of seeing John kneel to pray in the pulpit before he preached, in the scarlet cassock of a Queen's Chaplain under a gleaming white surplice. This was expository preaching of exceptional clarity and authority such as I had never heard.

John treated us as intelligent people. He trained us in 'thoughtful allegiance' to scripture. He moved us by his passion. He taught us 'double listening' – the need to 'hear' the word and the world and to find the connections. He abhorred in equal measure 'undevotional theology' (mind without heart) and 'untheological devotion' (heart without mind). He was, as he liked to say, 'an impenitent believer in the importance of biblical preaching'. We loved it!

Landmark sermon series here at All Souls on Romans, Ephesians, Acts, II Timothy, and on Issues Facing Christians, later travelled the world and formed the core of some of John's fifty-one, books. As we read those books now, we can still hear the structure of his delivery and the cadences of his voice. We would sometimes joke that John was clearer on the Apostle Paul than was the Apostle Paul![16]

His Honour, Judge David Turner *served as All Souls Churchwarden 1983-2006. Here he reflects back on his arrival in All Souls in 1972 as a first year law student at King's College, London.*

he urged me to be 'strong in truth and soft in love'

things 'of first importance'. Matters like church practice are all secondary. We teach students to unite around these primaries, hence the name 'Christian Union', by which campus groups are often known. The distinction between primary / secondary was instinctive to John Stott.[15] He was a peacemaker, eirenic, gracious; a listener. But he had an iron backbone. The essentials *were* essential. His book *The Cross of Christ*, which he considered his best, left no room for doubt.

Pulpits in reach of major universities will always be strategic places for the gospel. The number of evangelical ministers in university towns were few in the early days, but over the years, not least through the work of John Stott and the leaders of IVF/UCCF, the map changed. New generations of evangelicals, nurtured in the Christian Unions, were gradually filling pulpits.

John was a student at Ridley Hall when Tyndale House was established as a Centre for Biblical Research in 1944. His far-sightedness, even at that age, saw the future implications of this research centre, initiated by Douglas Johnson and his friends. In due course there would be evangelicals teaching in theology faculties of secular universities. Their influence would spill down into Christian publishing, into the local church, into the CUs, and so into the lives of students, soon to become Christian graduates in the public arenas. Forming the influencers of the next generation is a serious obligation for the Church.

In London in the 1960s and 1970s thousands of international students poured into Britain, especially from the former British colonies, now gaining independence. New governments wanted their future leaders to gain a western education. John Stott saw the vital role the UK evangelical church could play in building up Christian students, and in bringing the gospel to many who were not Christians. He established a position on his church staff to develop a specific ministry among international students.

John loved the secular university. While he saw some benefit for Christian students in enrolling in the US Christian colleges, it saddened him deeply that so many Christians were being segregated from the mainstream university. He enjoyed engaging with the humanists and the existentialists in university missions, and he loved the creativity shown by students in inviting people to meetings.[17] He urged that Christian students avoid the temptation to withdraw from university life. He referred to what he called 'rabbit hole Christianity'. Here Christians cut themselves off from the world, believing the only worthwhile activity is to evangelize or attend Christian meetings. Rabbits put their heads out of their burrows then, if there is no one about, race onto open land to catch their prey and swiftly return to their burrows. Christians can be like that, dashing to Christian activities, with minimal contact with the world. This breeds a hit-and-run form of evangelism that does not respect the integrity of a university, which, for all its student life excesses, is a community of learning.

John Stott urged students to develop what we might call 'a Christian mind', or a Christian worldview. That term was first coined by Professor Daniel Lamont in one of the early conferences of what was to

he referred to what be called 'rabbit-hole Christianity'

become the global IFES movement, in the 1930s. It has been popularised since by the writings of Harry Blamires and John Stott.[18] To develop a Christian mind fulfils three criteria. *First*, it glorifies our Creator who has made us as rational creatures in his own image and wants us to explore his revelation in nature and in scripture. *Secondly*, it enriches our Christian life as we can worship God only when we know who he is, and reflect on his glory. Faith rests on a knowledge of God's character. *Thirdly*, it strengthens our evangelistic witness. Many times in the Book of Acts we read of the apostles reasoning with people and seeking to persuade them. Faith and reason are not contrasted in scripture; it is faith and sight which are held in contrast.

Jesus challenged Thomas to believe 'having not seen', not 'having not thought'.

he remained a constant pastor to generations of leaders

While in his eighties, reflecting back, he said to me, 'If I could live my life again, I would join you in student ministry.' He stood with Charles Malik (and Martin Luther) as a man who took the university seriously.[19] Like Martyn Lloyd-Jones, John Stott remained close to the IFES student movements, and a constant pastor to its generations of leaders. We thank God for him.

Dr Lindsay Brown *is International Director of The Lausanne Movement and IFES Evangelist-at-Large, working to raise up a new generation of evangelists in Europe's universities. He served as IFES General Secretary 1991-2007.*

Urbana Student
Missions
Convention, 1967

John Stott accepted an invitation to return to Urbana for a final time in 2006, aged eighty-five. However his fall that autumn prevented this.

JOHN STOTT AS A MODEL OF BIBLICAL VALUES

John Stott became a mentor while I was still a university student, long before I met him, through borrowed books from my layman father's library. I first read his expositions to the Urbana Missions Conventions, and his exposition of Romans 5-8: *Men Made New*. Later there came a long list of books, especially the *Bible Speaks Today* series, which modelled Bible exposition for us younger preachers. One of his greatest contributions to the church, in my view, was the way he demonstrated the glory of Bible exposition.

I met John Stott personally for the first time while a student at Fuller Seminary in the mid-1970s. I went for every programme in his one-day visit. During a Question and Answer session, a student asked him about study habits. In an earlier era, he said, pastors spent the whole morning studying, but that was impractical now. Instead, we should squeeze in whatever time we could find during the day to study. Squeezing in study time became an ambition in my life. The next time I met Stott was in Singapore, when he spoke at The Lausanne Movement's Asian Leadership Conference on Evangelism (ALCOE, 1978). The first thing he asked me was, 'Are you finding time to study?'

squeezing in study time became an ambition in my life

At this conference someone asked

Despite all our Bible study aids, there is a woeful lack of biblical literacy. One reason is that preachers do not devote enough time for study, to apply the Bible effectively to issues facing us today. Stott devoted long hours to studying, and *applying* the word. His call to study is surely an urgent call for us now.

Ajith Fernando

29

about contextualization, which was just becoming a buzz word. Stott's response surprised us. Contextualization, he said, began with studying the Bible, and knowing it deeply. Then, he said, we should know our society, and apply the Bible in it. This was what came to be known as 'double listening'. His writing on key topics became definitive treatments. They were first and foremost biblical, and they applied biblical truth to contemporary society. They showed how biblical truth should be practised, and they engaged with controversial issues; another great contribution to the church.

I Believe in Preaching (US title *Between Two Worlds*, 1982) set a new standard for preaching. We are representatives of the great God in this world and must work hard at buttressing the presentation of God's truth both with accuracy and relevance. Then came *Issues Facing Christians Today* (1984) which looked at social and ethical issues, and went into several editions. My favourite is *The Cross of Christ* (1986), the most enriching theological book I have read. It is one of the few books on the cross which addresses questions non-Christians ask about the death of Christ.

For about four months I took *The Cross of Christ* with me wherever I went. I wrote copious notes in the margins, composed a detailed table of contents, and compiled my own topical index at the back. Once I was travelling home by bus from a camp in the mountains. It was a six-hour journey, and I had to stand as the bus was full, so could not read while the bus was moving. I read while I waited for the bus, and then reached for the book again from a rack above the seats each time the bus stopped to drop and pick up passengers. Suddenly someone said that a book had fallen out of the bus through the window. I knew it was my precious book, and took my bag and got off the bus to go in search of it. People on the road informed me that someone in a bus coming the other way had seen it fall, stopped their bus, and picked it up.

police let me get into the jeep, and we gave chase

As they explained this, a police jeep arrived. The police asked what had happened and, when they heard, let me get into the jeep, and we gave chase after the bus! We finally caught it up in the next town. I gratefully took possession of the book and proceeded on my journey. This was a book I could not afford to lose, with all its notes.

he lived out servanthood to bewildered emerging leaders

For Christians in Asia, the measures of effective leadership can bear trappings of earthly success - a huge audience, a luxurious house, an expensive car. A speaker may bring a large entourage and breeze in with a huge car or even by helicopter. He may have little personal contact with people. Stott was just the opposite. Yet even the secular media recognised this humble man as one of the most influential people of the twentieth century. He lived out servanthood to a bewildered generation of emerging Christians leaders.

My first visit to John Stott's home in London left a deep impression on me. Among the things in that spartan flat was a kneeler, where he prayed. One of the first questions he asked me was 'How is Jeyaraj?' Jeyaraj is a Youth for Christ staffworker in Sri Lanka, who was arrested on suspicion of terrorism, then released after fifteen months, without charges. He had an amazing ministry in prison. I had asked prayer for Jeyaraj in my six-monthly newsletter. Stott had not only been praying for him, but he also remembered his difficult name! Here he emulated Paul who prayed for a large number of people in different parts of the Christian world. A wide and large prayer list goes with being a servant of the global Church.

John Stott did not join those who used e-mail as their primary means of communication. Through a wide personal correspondence, he showed active concern for individuals. What a surprise it was for this 34-year-old unknown preacher to receive a copy of his book *I Believe in Preaching* personally inscribed, 'Ajith—friend and brother in the gospel of Christ, with esteem and affection. John Stott.' In later correspondence he called himself 'Uncle John'. His annual newsletter always included a personal note to me and my wife whom he mentioned by name, until it became too difficult for him to write personal notes. He would often respond to my six-monthly newsletter with a handwritten letter on an aerogramme. If I had mentioned a book I was hoping to write, he would send titles of books that would help me in preparing.

My friend Dr Peter Kuzmic once went to an airport chapel to pray. He saw the grey head of a man in the front of the chapel, arranging papers. It was John Stott, sorting through hundreds of letters. His published output alone was enormous. But he also wrote personal letters to *hundreds* of younger leaders, to encourage and instruct. Inspired by this I decided that if I am to have an international ministry, I too will need to spend considerable time in writing letters.

The Lausanne Younger Leaders Conference in Singapore in 1987 was a defining moment in many leaders' lives. I was on the organizing committee. John Stott expressed his desire to be there to encourage those attending. Most of the speakers were themselves younger leaders. We were happy to hear that he was coming, but could allot him only one talk. To me this seemed an embarrassing act of disrespect to an elder statesman. But he became the hero of the conference by not speaking! He stayed for all ten days just to be an encouragement

he stayed for all ten days just to encourage us

to us. Finding a quiet corner on the university campus where we met, he would sit and talk with people by appointment. I was one who benefited in that way.

During the late 1980s, Lausanne's chairman, Leighton Ford, was advocating that we be Kingdom seekers rather than empire builders. Stott exemplified this in Singapore and all through his life. He left no new structures to perpetuate his influence, because he was intent on strengthening existing structures. As Chris Wright shows us, the organization which emerged from his ministry, Langham Partnership, focuses on equipping other ministries rather than building its own structures.

John Stott's international ministry coincided with the shift of the centre of gravity of Christianity to the Majority World. This has not been a smooth transition. Many Majority World leaders felt that Western leaders did not even try to understand what they were saying. They suspected them of empire building. This gave rise to an almost racist animosity among some of the sharpest minds in the Majority World church towards Western church leadership. With Westerners like John Stott, and other Lausanne leaders Leighton Ford, John Reid, Jack Dain and Robert Coleman, who endeavoured to be servants to our churches, it was impossible for me to have my life sullied by angry thoughts towards Westerners.

it was impossible to have angry thoughts towards Westerners

John Stott truly exemplified servanthood to the world church. At a time when evangelicals are criticized as arrogant for insisting on the finality of Christ, no apologetic is as vital as a servant lifestyle.

Dr Ajith Fernando, *author and Bible teacher, is former Director, and now Teaching Director, Sri Lanka Youth for Christ. He is a special advisor to the Lausanne Theology Working Group.*

FRIENDSHIP, INFLUENCE AND THE FUTURE

John Stott's links with IFES movements around the world gave him unique access to some of the keenest up-and-coming minds, across the disciplines. He would hand-pick students and young graduates to look with him at some of the new frontiers. They included future lawyers and professors of bioethics, medicine and theology. With an eye to their later influence, he would draw them into discussions, to introduce them to academics and theologically-reflective practitioners whose credentials were already established. His vision was to equip the church to serve the nations. In this, friendship was central. Nigel Cameron, then one of those students, explains:[21]

'Friendship featured highly in all John Stott's ministry and dealings; he worked and he networked through friendship. This gift of friendship, combined with his interdisciplinary and enquiring mind, equipped him to bring traditional Christianity to bear on science, medicine, contemporary thinking about war and nuclear deterrence, and such big questions. He was perhaps uniquely able to convene that largely private discussion among the upper echelons of science and medicine and the armed forces... as he laboured mightily to bridge the Christian faith community and the hottest of emerging issues.

'It struck me then [in the 1970s], and does more forcefully now, how his network of personal friendships, which snaked across the face of the planet, was both embedded in his character, and was, more than anything else, the key to his astonishing influence. I'll treasure his bird book which he gave me when I last had tea with him. Simply the humblest human it was ever my privilege to meet.'

Prof Nigel M de S Cameron *was a student in Cambridge and Edinburgh universities in the 1970s. He is President of the Center for Policy on Emerging Technologies in Washington DC.*

JOHN STOTT AND
THE CHURCH OF ENGLAND

John Stott was baptized, confirmed and ordained as a loyal and lifelong member of the Church of England. It was an Anglican church, All Souls, Langham Place, where he attended as a child and went on to serve as assistant curate, Rector and Rector-Emeritus through all his ministry. His funeral service was held in All Souls, and the Thanksgiving Service in St Paul's, the cathedral of the Diocese of London, his 'home diocese' for all his ninety years.

He was never a Prebendary of St Paul's as other All Souls rectors have been, never a member of the Church of England General Synod, never a bishop. But two of our most distinguished contemporary church historians, David Edwards and Adrian Hastings,[22] have given their assessments in unmistakeable terms. David Edwards described him as, apart from Archbishop William Temple, 'the most influential clergyman in the Church of England during the twentieth century'. He places John Stott, therefore, firmly in the Anglican scene, and is right to do so.

One has only to think of the structures that John Stott created to fulfil his vision of a renewed evangelicalism. Consider the Evangelical Fellowship in the Anglican Communion, the Church of England Evangelical Council, the great National Evangelical Anglican Congresses of 1967 and 1977. Again and again, sometimes privately and sometimes publicly, we find John Stott taking a lead for Scriptural standards in the affairs of the Church of England: heading a delegation to the Archbishops over Reservation of the Sacrament, or offering cogent comments on the Anglican/Roman Catholic Agreed Statements, or sustaining a continuing critique of the Anglican/Methodist proposals for reunion, or the major liturgical revisions of the 1960s and 1970s.

His commitment to the church of his baptism, and his concern for many younger evangelical clergy who looked to him for leadership, is what lay behind the confrontation between Dr Martyn Lloyd-Jones as speaker and John Stott as chairman of the National Assembly of Evangelicals in October 1966. John Stott felt bound to use (some felt, to misuse) his position in the chair to resist a call by the speaker for

among John Stott's heroes was Charles Simeon

his hearers, 'especially the ministers and clergy' among them, to leave the major denominations and form a united church.

Among John Stott's heroes was Charles Simeon, the Anglican divine, minister of Holy Trinity Church, Cambridge from 1783 to 1836, whose mark is on Cambridge still. John Stott edited an anthology of Simeon's sermons, for Simeon, like John Stott, was first and foremost a man of the Scriptures; but they also shared a love for their church. Simeon is well-known for declaring that 'the finest sight short of heaven would be a whole congregation using the prayers of the Liturgy in the true spirit of them.' John Stott was to write in the 1960s about a proposed Prayer Book revision, that the *Book of Common Prayer* (still substantially as Simeon knew it) was 'a precious heritage', and its Holy Communion service 'deeply satisfying to the hearts and minds of generations of churchmen'. Twenty years later he wrote, 'I am deeply grateful to be a member and a minister' of the Church of England, 'and to be able to remain such with good conscience.' He was by no means blind to his church's faults and shortcomings (which he explored in the same article) but while the Church of England remained in its formularies a church loyal to Scripture, he was thankful to continue as a loyal member.

Adrian Hastings, Professor of Theology at the University of Leeds, affirmed that John Stott 'must be accounted one of the most influential figures in the Christian world, standing as he did at the point of intersection of the Evangelical movement and the Church of England'. That phrase 'point of intersection' reminds us that John Stott, both in England and on the world stage, was an Anglican evangelical rather than an evangelical Anglican. This distinction is so crucial that it is best to quote John Stott's own summary of his position. It begins his chapter, *I believe in the Church of England* in Gavin Reid (ed) *Hope for the Church of England?* [23]

> Let me begin by spelling out my priorities. First and foremost, by God's sheer mercy, I am a Christian seeking to follow Jesus Christ. Next, I am an evangelical Christian because of my conviction that evangelical principles (especially sola scriptura and sola gratia) are integral to authentic Christianity, and that to be an evangelical Christian is to be a New Testament Christian, and vice versa. Thirdly, I am an Anglican evangelical Christian, since the Church of England is the particular historical tradition or denomination to which I belong. But I am not an Anglican first, since denominationalism is hard to defend. It seems to me correct to call oneself an Anglican evangelical (in which evangelical is the noun and Anglican the descriptive adjective) rather than an evangelical Anglican (in which Anglican is the noun and evangelical the adjective).

The evidence for this is not far to seek. It can be seen in his writing (some fifty books and many articles and papers), almost all of which cross denominational and geographical divides, uniting those concerned to understand Scripture and to follow Jesus Christ as Lord. Again, consider John Stott's involvement with a huge range of interdenominational societies and movements: Scripture Union, UCCF, IFES, Evangelical Alliance,

an Anglican evangelical rather than an evangelical Anglican

Tearfund, Bible Society, his own Evangelical Literature Trust, and the whole of The Lausanne Movement for World Evangelization. Or think of the great university missions. Their aim was to win men and women for Christ, not for any church affiliation. And in his ceaseless missionary journeys overseas, John Stott could be found teaching the Bible under Baptist auspices in Eastern Europe or in the Mar Thoma church in India, as readily as in the Episcopalian context in Australia.

In his celebrated book of broadcast talks *Mere Christianity*,[24] C S Lewis wrote of himself:

> The reader should be warned that I offer no help to anyone who is hesitating between two Christian 'denominations'. You will not learn from me whether you ought to become an Anglican, a Methodist, a Presbyterian... This omission is intentional (even in the list I have just given the order is alphabetical). There is no mystery about my own position. I am a very ordinary layman of the Church of England.'

Apart from 'layman', those who read John Stott's legacy in print today will find that, with few exceptions, he could say much the same. Not invariably so, perhaps (remember that 'point of intersection') but very nearly so.

And now, of course, those issues are behind him. I do not know whether John Stott knew the story of George Whitefield in Philadelphia, but I expect he did. David Edwards tells how Whitefield was preaching from a balcony when he looked upwards and cried out 'Father Abraham, whom have you in heaven? Any Episcopalians? Presbyterians? Independents or Seceders? Have you any Methodists? And the answer came, according to Whitefield: 'We don't know those names here.'

The Rt Revd Timothy Dudley-Smith, *retired Bishop of Thetford, authorized biographer, and long-time friend of John Stott from Cambridge days, preached at the memorial service in St Paul's Cathedral.*

AN ENCOURAGEMENT TO THE LOCAL CHURCH IN WALES

John Stott travelled the world as a teacher, preacher and evangelist, but a little corner of Pembrokeshire, South West Wales, held a special place in his affection. The Hookses, one-time farmhouse, whose land had been requisitioned for a wartime airfield, was home from home for about three months each year. While in seclusion there he wrote most of his books, but he also found time to support the local church.

He regularly attended worship in the local parish church, along with guests at The Hookses. This was much appreciated by the local people.

In the 1950s and 60s evangelicals were few and far between in the Church in Wales, virtually an endangered species, and generally regarded as being non-conformists at heart and not true Anglicans. John was concerned

evangelicals were virtually an endangered species

about this, and he resolved to 'do something about it'. He lobbied the Archbishop, but he also decided to invite the few evangelicals known to him to an annual day of teaching and fellowship at The Hookses; some drove a hundred miles to find an oasis of spiritual blessing in barren times. Out of those meetings was founded the Evangelical Fellowship in the Church in Wales (EFCW) in March 1967, of which I was the first secretary, with 28 members. For thirty years or more the 'Dale Days' were a constant source of encouragement and affirmation, and helped members of EFCW to play an increasingly significant part in the life of the Church in Wales.

In 1970 John offered to give a lecture on 'An unchanging gospel in a changing world' for the ministers and clergy of Pembrokeshire. The Bishop was invited to chair the meeting: he was new in post, very much an Anglo-Catholic, and rather suspicious of anything evangelical. He accepted with some hesitation, met John over lunch, listened to a gracious, brilliant and highly-relevant lecture, and his whole attitude changed. Prejudice is overcome, not by argument or criticising one another from the safety of entrenched positions, but by gracious engagement on a personal level.

I, along with many others, have good reason to be grateful to John for his books, his teaching and his constant encouragement of ministry in the local church. One special memory I have is of the time he came to preach for me in St Giles, Letterston in 1971. His sermon was a clear and winsome exposition of the gospel, but the thing which impressed me most was to watch him in the after-church 'bun fight', wandering around, cup of tea in hand, speaking to as many of the village people as possible, following the example of Jesus, as 'one who came, not to be served, but to serve'.

BURIAL IN WALES

Bill Lewis, one of John Stott's oldest friends in Pembrokeshire, led the service for the interment of ashes, in the church of St James the Great, Dale. John asked for the following words to be inscribed on a gravestone of Welsh slate.

Buried here are the ashes of
JOHN R. W. STOTT
(1921-2011)
Rector of All Souls Church
Langham Place, London
1950-1975
Rector Emeritus 1975-2011
Who resolved
Both as the ground of his salvation
And as the subject of his ministry
To know nothing except
JESUS CHRIST
And him crucified
(1 Corinthians 2:2)

PASTOR, LEADER AND FRIEND

Soon after I arrived in the village, the wife of the local Squire, on my first pastoral visit, had asked me whom I thought 'worth knowing'. (My answer to this question would have been 'about a thousand people' *ie* the whole population.) Then she suggested the name of the Justice of the Peace. He happened to be a very faithful church member, whom I already knew. As I already knew him, I became kosher! How different was our guest preacher; to him everyone in the room was worth knowing!

John decided that his final earthly resting place should be the village cemetery in Dale

In 2005, six years before his death, John decided to invite ministers and clergy from Pembrokeshire to a day of teaching at The Hookses, twice a year; this was attended by up to thirty grateful people. A few times he spoke himself, though frail, and this spoke volumes about faithfulness to the end. The mantle for this, as with several other ministries, has fallen on Chris Wright.

Christians in Pembrokeshire find it very moving that John decided that his final earthly resting place should be the village cemetery in Dale, about half a mile from The Hookses.

Revd Bill Lewis, *now retired, spent 35 years in parish ministry, and served for five years as Provincial Officer for Evangelism and Adult Education in the Church in Wales.*

A VISION FOR
WHOLE-LIFE DISCIPLESHIP

John was 61 years old when The London Institute for Contemporary Christianity (LICC) was founded. At that point in his life he could instead have pastored a church, or taught in almost any seminary or theological college in the world. He could have concentrated only on his global itinerant preaching and teaching ministry, or accepted an episcopal call, with a seat in the House of Lords. But instead he chose to focus much energy around this new, small institute for contemporary Christianity

John and a few friends[25] saw with searing clarity how hard evangelicals found it to apply the word of God to issues we encounter. Evangelical preaching was beset by the sacred-secular divide, which left pastors and lay people with a narrow concept of mission, and a narrow vision for discipleship and disciple-making. One of John's major contributions to this area shortly after the London Institute was founded is his book *Issues Facing Christians Today* (IVP).[26]

The LICC faculty gave lectures on the hot topics of the era, and sought to engage with pressing concerns.[27] At the heart of LICC was 'whole-life discipleship'. Its unique ten-week residential course, 'The Christian in the Modern World' (CMW), combined listening to the word and the world: understanding culture, mission and discipleship.

The CMW course brought together Christians from a whole variety of walks of life, and from every continent – lawyers, doctors, business people, pastors, cross-cultural missionaries, para-church workers. The result was a wonderfully vibrant mix of people who were helped to think outside the confines of their own culture. Together they were compelled to recognise that the Bible needed to be applied beyond the church and their local culture, to every sphere of life.

he never elevated his own calling above any other

Today, you can see the fruit of that course in the lives of its alumni, who have gone on to make a significant impact for Christ. Some have founded variations of LICC in their own countries.

John was one of the greatest preachers of his generation, but he never elevated his own calling above any other. He was interested in raising up a new generation of missional Christian disciples in every area of life, not just a new generation of preachers.

He taught and wrote and preached at All Souls and all round the world, and he also discipled. Most of his study assistants, disciples by any other name, pursued a preaching and teaching ministry. But John saw discipling in a much wider context. For example he met with a group of business people in London for a regular prayer breakfast. And he met with young professionals in diverse fields to engage biblically with the key books, films, exhibitions, events. He listened carefully to everyone but, as one of them put it, 'he was really teaching us to engage with culture.'

John was essentially a disciple-maker. He was making disciples for ministry in the church, for ministry in business, for ministry in every area of life. This is a goal and a practice that very few

John was essentially a disciple-maker

church leaders have emulated. The inseparability of proclaiming the gospel and practically pursuing social justice has now been grasped in principle by large sections of the global evangelical church. But there is more work to do in helping to equip the laity for whole-life mission and whole-life discipleship.

The mission strategy of most churches is focused around people using leisure time to join missionary initiatives led by church-paid workers. This vital part of the mission of God has borne much fruit, but is only one part of the whole.

Mark Greene

John recruited a rich mix of people to come to LICC for the CMW course. He taught double-listening: listening to the word and listening to the world. But the course actually engaged in triple listening: listening to the word, listening to the world, and listening to one another in humility, seeking to help one another fulfil our diverse callings, individual and corporate, in the diverse settings where God has placed us. A teacher, lawyer or a mechanic should go to work with a sense of representing the body of Christ, supported in prayer and fellowship, and able to draw on the wisdom of a local body of believers, to the glory of the Father.

the course actually engaged in triple listening

It was a radical vision back in 1982, and it still is. LICC's team is now

JOHN STOTT: ORNI-THEOLOGIAN

John Stott's father would take him on walks as a small boy, to teach him how to observe the natural world, in which he built an informed interest. 'Shut your mouth and open your eyes and ears,' his father would say.

His first interest, as a small boy under his father's tutelage, was in butterflies. One day his sister, Joy, threw a cushion at him in the nursery. It missed him, landing instead on his painstakingly-mounted butterfly collection, built with care, pride and love. It was beyond repair, and John was inconsolable.

Looking back years later, he reflected that (i) he had probably provoked Joy into throwing the cushion, so it was partly his fault; and (ii) this was what steered him in the direction of birdwatching, for which he became very thankful. 'People think one is eccentric enough to go round the world with binoculars,' he remarked, adding with a grin. 'To have gone round the world with a butterfly net would have been much too much to bear.'

much larger and our range of activity broader, but the focus remains the same as that of our founders – namely envisioning and equipping God's people, lay and ordained, for whole-life mission. Will you join us?

Mark Greene, *Executive Director of the London Institute for Contemporary Christianity, is former Vice Principal of the London School of Theology; he spent ten years in the advertising industry.*

John Stott was one of the world's experts in birds. His desk at The Hookses looked over West Dale Bay, and his binoculars were always close to hand. He personally sighted 2,500 of the world's 9,000 bird species. His missionary journeys included time for birdwatching, and friends were drawn into the hobby through his passion. Poetically, his purchase of The Hookses in 1954 was from Peter Conder, then Warden of Skokholm island, a world-famous breeding ground and bird observatory about five miles offshore from Dale. Peter Conder had owned the property only briefly, and was moving to London to take up the position of Director of the Royal Society for the Protection of Birds (RSPB).

In 1999 *The Birds, our Teachers* was published: subtitled *Essays in Orni-theology* for which he took all the photographs himself. Later editions included a DVD of his 70th birthday trip to the Galapagos islands, and his own narration of the book script. This book contains eleven truths of the Christian life, illustrated through the behaviour of birds. The title was inspired by Martin Luther's comment on the Sermon on the Mount: 'Let the little birds be your theologians'.

VOICES OF APPRECIATION FROM AFRICA

'Uncle John's parish extended to Francophone Africa'

John Stott loved Francophone Africa and visited several countries in the region. At a time of harsh ethnic conflict, he travelled to both Rwanda and Burundi in the Great Lakes region and brought much encouragement to believers there. As an untiring ambassador for students, he spoke with church leaders in support of the GBU, underlining the strategic nature of this movement. I remember the impact of his visit on the churches and on the GBU students.

In fact church leaders and other Christians across Francophone African have been profoundly influenced by this pastor and evangelical theologian, not least through his books. The first one I read was *L'essentiel du Christianisme (Basic Christianity)*, while a student in Togo. In our Bible study group, we were looking for books which would engage with fellow students and help us to articulate our faith. We wanted to offer our non-believing friends a book which was clear and intellectually rigorous, and which would summarise evangelical Christianity.

His short book, *Plaidoyer pour une foi intelligente (Your Mind Matters)*, helped countless students and francophone African intellectuals to articulate their faith intelligently. Through this John Stott made a lasting contribution. He urged us not to neglect our intellect as we live out our faith.

John Stott's views on evangelism and social action, on showing respect for cultures, on openness to dialogue, and his major work *Le chrétien et les défis de la vie moderne (Issues Facing Christians Today)* have been widely influential in Francophone Africa. Readers of these works heard an echo of a Christian faith which fully embraces the non-Western world.

Towards the end of his life, Francophone Africa received another benefit of John Stott's ministry, through his concern to develop expository preaching. Over the last few years, Langham Preaching seminars have been held in several countries including Côte d'Ivoire, Benin and Burkina Faso.

John Stott was also a remarkably faithful friend. He valued people and encouraged them in their faith. He never forgot me after our first meeting, and he prayed for me. In 1999, knowing I was a biologist, he inscribed a copy of his book *The Birds Our Teachers* and sent it to me in Abidjan, Côte d'Ivoire.

When I was called to my current role as General Secretary of IFES, Uncle John invited me to visit him, with Lindsay Brown, from whom I was taking over. At that time, in the summer of 2007, Uncle John was recovering from a

while confined to bed, he received us with great enthusiasm

fall and confined to bed, but he received us with great enthusiasm. He gave me several pieces of advice, one of which was the need to affirm the uniqueness of Jesus in a pluralist world. He prayed for me and for the ministry of IFES. It was a very significant moment for me, to be sent out with the prayer of this elder brother, model and mentor. I was still waiting to move with my family from Abidjan to Oxford, to take up my new role, and Uncle John lent help by writing to the British government, to request that they grant me the needed permissions.

Uncle John's parish extended to Francophone Africa. We give thanks to God for his life of service and his humility which always pointed people to the cross of Jesus.

Dr Daniel Bourdanné, *General Secretary of IFES, served as IFES Regional Secretary for Francophone Africa and as an International Deputy Director of The Lausanne Movement.*

What I learned from Uncle John Stott

I first heard of the Revd Dr John Stott while I was a student in Ahmadu Bello University, in Zaria, Nigeria, in the 1970s. We first met in Chicago in 1986, when I was studying at Wheaton Graduate School, and from those days I began to know him as a friend. He was deeply committed to nurturing a younger generation of leaders for the church, particularly in the non-Western world. For many of us in Africa, Uncle John was first a friend and then a mentor. My story is not unique; Uncle John gave generously of himself to those he got to know. Let me share three things I learnt from him.

> *Uncle John was first a friend and then a mentor*

First, From before I met him, Uncle John taught me that my mind matters. I began student ministry with NIFES in 1980 as a young graduate, armed with what I had learnt in the Christian fellowship on campus, and my sociology degree. Soon afterwards I read Uncle John's book *Your Mind Matters*. It changed my attitude and disposition towards biblical scholarship; up to then I felt all that mattered was the Holy Spirit. Uncle John taught me that using my mind was as important as walking in, and working with, the Holy Spirit.

With his encouragement, I have studied Christian history and theology. He suggested I pursue a doctorate at Aberdeen University, after I finished at Wheaton Graduate School. The very same week that I received the offer of a Langham Scholarship, I also received an invitation to return to Nigeria to serve as NIFES General Secretary. What a dilemma to choose. Uncle John encouraged me to follow my conviction; he promised that the scholarship would be kept open, should I decide to serve in NIFES first. I returned to Nigeria, and served in NIFES before later studying for a Masters in Theology at the University of Edinburgh. To congratulate me on completing my Masters, Uncle John sent me a copy of *Birds of West Africa*. Today, by God's grace, I'm a beneficiary of a Langham scholarship once more, this time for doctoral studies.

Second, Uncle John was clearly concerned about issues facing the church on the African continent. In 1999 Bishop David Zac Niringiye and I started the Institute of Christian Impact for

I can in my own way emulate the values I learnt

IFES in English- and Portuguese-speaking Africa.[29] Uncle John delivered the inaugural address in Kampala. He also gave a public lecture, attended by most members of the Ugandan House of Parliament. He challenged us to be bold in our Christian witness in the public arena. In addition, he has empowered the church in Africa through the threefold ministry of The Langham Partnership.[30] Through his own books he has left us a library to help us engage with issues in the church and in society.

Thirdly, Uncle John's life taught me humility. When I visited him in his pad for tea, after preaching at All Souls in February 2006, I was struck with the depth of his humility. We talked over aspects of life and ministry, then he asked me to pray for him, and without the slightest hesitation he went on his knees. As we knelt and prayed together, I was overwhelmed by both his humility, and his intimacy with God.

The opportunity to know and interact with Uncle John has had significant impact on my life and ministry: within Nigeria, around Africa, and now in my present global role. I will never be an Uncle John, but I can in my own way emulate the values I learnt from him.

Revd Femi B Adeleye *serves as IFES Associate General Secretary for Partnership and Collaboration. He was a plenary speaker at The Third Lausanne Congress.*

JOHN STOTT: GOD'S GIFT TO THE CHURCH IN LATIN AMERICA

John Stott has left a deep mark on the Protestant communities of Latin America. There are good memories of his many visits from the first in 1974, (Mexico, Perú, Chile and Argentina) to the last in 2001 (Lima, Perú). *Basic Christianity* appeared in Spanish in 1959, and since then twenty-six of his books have been translated and published in Spanish, and a good number in Portuguese; some reprinted several times. He is equally appreciated among Pentecostals and Presbyterians, among Baptists and Methodists, and among Lutherans and the vast number of independent churches that make up the growing Protestant people in this part of the world.

Let me start with student work, my own sphere of ministry for 26 years all over Latin America. *Basic Christianity* was an excellent tool - for communicating the gospel at university level, and for students who had committed their lives to Christ. During John Stott's visits, we usually tried to get senior student leaders to his Bible expositions and seminars. He was very good in dialogues that followed, and very precise in answers to questions. He also participated in, and enjoyed, celebrations, so students felt he was close to them. Several generations found the Spanish version of *Your mind matters* a liberating experience, because fundamentalist missionaries had left behind a kind of anti-intellectual bias. René Padilla got the best translator in the publishing community to translate it in 1974.

> *students felt he was close to them*

We were committed to making Bible exposition central in our training programs. We wanted growing churches to be able to enjoy it and practise it. Stott's exposition did not lose its force in translation. I have in my memory the picture of Peruvian, Argentinian and Mexican students absorbed as they listened, and at the end exclaiming 'That is the kind of preacher I want to be!'

In 1969 we held the First Latin American Congress of Evangelism in Bogotá, Colombia. Here a group of evangelists, pastors, seminary faculty and lay leaders decided to found a fellowship to encourage theological reflection which was both evangelical and relevant to our context. The

his model of Bible exposition was greatly needed in our churches

following year the Latin American Theological Fraternity (FTL) was founded. Some of its members (such as René Padilla, Orlando Costas, Peter Savage, Emilio Antonio Núñez and me) were speakers at the 1974 Lausanne Congress on World Evangelization. John Stott chaired the drafting committee for *The Lausanne Covenant*. We knew this guaranteed that voices from the Majority World would be heard. His global ministry was making him sensitive to the concerns of a new generation of evangelical leaders, and to the traditional paternalism of the West. Over the decades that followed, Stott modeled servant-leadership in The Lausanne Movement.

During his visits to Latin America (several of them coordinated by the FTL or the evangelical student movements), we would intentionally invite pastors and missionaries who were not related to these bodies, because his model of Bible exposition was greatly needed in our churches. When the FTL was founded in 1970, its Cochabamba Declaration stated: 'Preaching is often void of biblical substance. The evangelical pulpit is in a state of crisis. We find among ourselves a depressing ignorance of the Bible and of the application of its message to today's needs. The biblical message is indisputably pertinent to Latin Americans, but its proclamation does not play the part it should among us.'[31] We were committed to changing this.

a new generation of Bible expositors were schooled under Stott's ministry

Stott supported us in this effort

and always encouraged us. There is now a new generation of Bible expositors, who, in one way or other, were schooled under Stott's ministry.[32] Angelit Guzmán was with him in Cuba in 1996 and she took some of his expositions and edited them for publication with pieces written by Jorge Atiencia and myself under the title *Así leo la Biblia*.[33] We wrote about applying the Bible in our lives, and how to prepare Bible expositions. Now expositors from several generations have made contributions to the one volume Latin American Bible Commentary.[34]

he would not give up an inch on his firm convictions

His status as an Anglican minister active in his church has been of help to Latin Americans who had a strong anti-Roman Catholic bias, coming from both their evangelical convictions and their experience as a persecuted religious minority in Latin America. His personal stance as an evangelical taking part in the Evangelical-Roman Catholic Dialogue on Mission was an eye-opener to many; some were at first shocked or surprised by his participation. The Report he co-edited with Monsignor Basil Meeking shows his openness to dialogue, his recognition of a wide common ground and at the same time his firm convictions from which he would not give up an inch.[35] Among evangelicals in Latin America and southern Europe there is still a long way to go in terms of defining a mature attitude in relation to Roman Catholicism and issues of ecumenism. I think that Stott's ecclesiology, if adequately identified and expounded, could be a great help.

Stott's commitment to an evangelicalism that is faithful to its basic convictions, but not sectarian or narrow-minded, was a great gift to the church universal during the second part of the twentieth century. His ability to mediate creatively between positions that were sometimes exaggerated or intolerant required a good measure of patience, openness and self-control as well as a good command of words. These gifts were evident in his contributions to The Lausanne Movement. The depth, quality and clarity of documents such as *The*

Lausanne Covenant (1974), the *Willowbank Report on Gospel and Culture* (1978) or the *Grand Rapids Report on Gospel and Social Responsibility* (1982) owe much to his hard work as both a chair person and a writer.[36] We Latin Americans have added the cultural and national biases of our own background to the

his ability to mediate required patience, openness and self-control

divisiveness received from the European or North American missionary heritage. So the evangelical enterprise is far from being an easy road to walk. For those of us that worked with Stott in global projects, his example was a great blessing and inspiration, as well as a model we tried to follow.

Through these years I have also witnessed the role of John Stott as an encourager. In some gatherings were missionaries or pastors who faced critical situations. Stott always offered an attentive ear. His emphasis on a missionary lifestyle modeled after the pattern of Jesus could have been difficult for some to hear. But he knew how to offer clear teaching from the front about Christ's demands, while also offering personal counsel in private conversation. For me, it was only through his continual encouragement that I adopted the discipline of setting apart time for writing, just as I took specific time for speaking engagements.[37]

In conversation, one could perceive how much John Stott had changed as a result of his international trips, and his encounters with other cultures and other parts of the church. As I think back to the drafting of *The Lausanne Covenant*, I remember the moment he coined the final sentence of paragraph 10: 'Christ's evangelists must humbly seek to empty themselves of all but their personal authenticity in order to become the servants of others, and churches must seek to transform and enrich culture, all for the glory of God.' What rich, careful, and perceptive words.

You can listen to John Stott's presentation of *The Lausanne Covenant* on the last full day of the 1974 Congress at www.lausanne.org. He and his drafting team of Hudson Armerding and myself, assisted by J D Douglas and Leighton Ford, invited comments at each stage of the process. We received hundreds, which were all translated and carefully considered. It was a finely-tuned and meticulous process. *The Covenant* truly reflected the mood of the Lausanne Congress as well as any single document could.

> *he did not come across as the typical British gentleman*

When he came to minister in Latin America, he did his best to put into practice that Christlike form of ministry. He did not come across as the typical British gentleman. He left behind some attitudes of class and nationality, and learned much along the way, not only in terms of food, simple lifestyle, or siesta time, but also in terms of theology. This is evident, for instance, in the second part of his book *The Incomparable Christ* (2001). And that is another reason why his books will continue being enjoyed, and transforming lives, in Latin America.

Prof Samuel Escobar, *from Peru, was a speaker at Lausanne 1974. After his 26 years with IFES in Latin America, he taught at Palmer Theological Seminary, Philadelphia. He is now retired in Valencia, Spain.*

JOHN STOTT AND THE LAUSANNE MOVEMENT

As decades pass, history will further unfold the extent of John Stott's influence on theological thinking, on preaching, on the tensions between the gospel and culture, on the development of a Christian mind, on evangelical commitment to social justice, and supremely on world evangelization.

His relationship with Lausanne,[38] particularly in the period 1974-1996 could well be described as reciprocal, even symbiotic. His multi-faceted ministry fitted the multi-faceted Lausanne aspirations, which he had played no small part in fashioning. Lausanne channels and networks would become a major means through which he brought influence to the church globally.

his relationship with Lausanne could be described as reciprocal, even symbiotic

In 2006, Doug Birdsall invited John Stott to accept a lifetime title of Honorary Chairman, which he did, with a sense of pleasure. It had been a consistent pattern to accept honorary titles only if he could maintain a lively link with the endeavour, and he followed news of planning for the Third Lausanne Congress with eager interest. Lindsay Brown was appointed as Lausanne Movement International Director in 2007, and Chris Wright, who followed in John's own stead as chair of the Lausanne Theology Working Group,[39] were both old friends.

His personal friendship with Billy Graham from the time of the Cambridge University mission in 1955 drew John Stott into the early stages of planning for the 1974 International Congress on World Evangelization, held in Lausanne, Switzerland, and from which city the Movement would take its name. He was by this stage already regarded as a leader and figurehead, through participation in World Council of Churches events, and in the 1966 conference on world evangelism in Berlin. The 1970s included seven or eight

Lausanne was to have a lion's share of his time

other international conferences. But from 1974, Lausanne was to have a lion's share of his time.

Edinburgh 1910 – learning from history

The world missions conference in Edinburgh, in June 1910, convened by John R Mott, a visionary from the US Mid-West with a deep passion for evangelism, was a remarkable gathering by any criteria. But from the outset it was flawed through well-intentioned but ill-considered decisions. In a move to gain the participation of the then Archbishop of Canterbury, Randall Thomas Davidson, John Mott agreed that matters of doctrine would not be discussed. It was a costly error of judgment. He opened his final address: 'The end of the congress is the beginning of the conquest', and participants left on this stirring note, resolved to give their best energy to the glory of Christ in world evangelization. The two world wars would have a huge bearing on mission strategy. But the unforeseen hidden cost for including the Archbishop was regarded by John Stott as having even more profound, and longer-lasting, significance.

As central questions on the content of the gospel, the theology of evangelism and the nature of the church were not on the agenda, Edinburgh 1910 proved a lost opportunity to engage with the critical theological challenges of the day. Theological liberalism was to dominate in university faculties and in seminaries for the next several decades. As a result, mission became sidelined in the church.[40]

Guarding Edinburgh's intended legacy

While the World Council of Churches, constituted in 1948, traces its roots back to Edinburgh 1910, there is a sense in which Lausanne is the 'spiritual legacy' of that conference, taking forward John Mott's true aspirations.

In Lausanne 1974, clear action was taken in the formation of the Programme to reclaim what had been intended. This can be seen in the strength of the speaker list, and also in John Stott's first plenary address, on 'The biblical basis of evangelism'. Thirty-five years later, in 2009, the matter was still clearly on Stott's mind. Doug Birdsall and Lindsay Brown conferred with him on several occasions as the Congress was being planned. He said he felt ashamed that leaders in his own communion had refused to discuss doctrinal issues for fear of division. It had rendered John Mott's rallying cry as delegates left Edinburgh severely weakened. 'You cannot speak of the gospel of Christ and the mission of the church without reflecting on biblical truth,' he said.

Lindsay Brown's Closing Address in Cape Town would leave no doubt about the clarity of vision and hope for Lausanne. The Congress was to sound 'a ringing re-affirmation of the uniqueness of Christ and the truth of the biblical gospel and a crystal clear statement on the mission of the church - all rooted in Scripture.' To launch a movement without biblical consensus was, he said, 'folly'. *The Cape Town Commitment* drew evangelicals together around its biblical indicatives before moving on to its gospel imperatives. Chris Wright engaged with John Stott on the way those biblical indicatives should be crafted.[41] But let us not rush ahead.

1974 A Congress and a Covenant

John Stott's reputation for clear theological thinking, his breadth of sympathy within the evangelical tradition,[42] and his gracious dealings with those of different persuasions, made him an obvious first choice to lead the process of crafting *The Lausanne Covenant*.

The Lausanne Covenant, which reflected the voices of the 1974 Congress, was adopted as a basis for hundreds of collaborative ventures over the rest of the century, and came to be regarded as one of the most significant documents in modern church history.[43] Social justice, too-long identified as a concern only for adherents to 'a social gospel' was now declared a biblical responsibility for evangelical Christians. This proved a watershed moment for the church. Realizing the

social justice was now declared a biblical responsibility

seriousness, of *The Lausanne Covenant*, John Stott worked on an exposition and commentary, published in 1975. It would, he sensed, be critical for the *Covenant* to be read and studied by individuals and groups.[44] His Preface, modestly written, does not record the intense pressure of working through nights to ensure all comments received from the participants were given proper consideration. It was a mammoth operation to translate them in a timely manner, but vital for the voices of the whole evangelical church to be heard.

The name 'Covenant' was carefully chosen. This was a covenant with God himself, and a covenant between all those who wanted to adopt it. The banner on the stage, in six languages, had proclaimed 'Let the Earth hear His Voice'; for that to happen, the whole evangelical church needed to work together.

THE LAUSANNE COVENANT

The Lausanne Covenant was 'prophetic' in the sense of speaking in a way which applied the word of God to the realities of the hour. And it retains its relevance and challenge now, and indeed for generations to come...

May its creative combinations of confidence and humility, of human energy and trust in God, of vision and realism, of joy in the Lord's doings and grief over our human failures, of strategic thinking and the Spirit's leading, of global vision and local action, of words and works – always remain characteristic of The Lausanne Movement, as they are of its Covenant.

Christopher J H Wright [45]

In July 1989 John Stott led the crafting team for *The Manila Manifesto* in The Second Lausanne Congress (Manila, Philippines), which in 31 Clauses built on and elaborated *The Lausanne Covenant*. This Congress took place a month after what the Chinese government termed the 'Tiananmen Incident', and just three months before the dismantling of the Berlin Wall. It drew 3,000 participants from 170 countries including Eastern Europe and the Soviet Union, but sadly none from China. Lausanne II in Manila [as it became known] was the catalyst for over 300 partnerships and new initiatives, in the developing world and elsewhere.

Five years before Lausanne II, John Stott completed his new and groundbreaking book *Issues Facing Christians Today*. This was a major contribution to evangelical thinking. It covered nuclear issues, pluralism, human rights, industrialization, sexual issues... It became a handbook for pastors and thinking church members, It was, he said, his 'contribution to the catching-up process' since the church was 'recovering from its temporarily-mislaid social conscience'. *The Lausanne Covenant* was continuing to create waves, reawakening a social conscience which had lain dormant in many quarters for perhaps two generations. The Lord Jesus had commissioned the apostles to teach new disciples 'everything' he had commanded them. This had plainly not been done. In God's grace, John Stott and The Lausanne Movement would become a means of re-establishing significant aspects of Christian duty.

Forming a Movement from a Congress

After the 1974 Congress, a Continuation Committee was set up, to build on what had been achieved. In January 1975 this group met in Mexico City with Bishop Jack Dain in the chair. There was considerable support for Billy Graham to become President of the new Lausanne Committee for World Evangelization, as it was then named. John Stott urged that this not be allowed to happen, or that there be several Co-Presidents. Billy Graham had already articulated his preference that the Movement adopt a narrower brief of what we could call Proclamation evangelism. If this were followed, the Movement would reflect neither the scriptural mandate of the church to be salt and light, nor its historical roots. On the strength of their 20-year friendship, John Stott, while hating discord, felt the need to speak. Jack Dain was in

John Stott, while hating discord, felt the need to speak

agreement, while others could not bring themselves to voice anything other than blind allegiance to Billy Graham, given his worldwide stature. Some perceived it as a power struggle. Billy Graham saw his mistake in yielding to pressure to accept the role. John Stott was asked to be on the drafting committee to prepare a statement on the progress of the meetings, which was accepted with only minor amendments. He described this in his diary as 'a helpful note of unanimity on which to conclude a rather traumatic conference.'[46]

When the Committee met the following year in Atlanta, four separate functions were identified as being needed to achieve the Movement's aim: (i) Intercession (ii) Theology and Education (iii) Strategy (iv) Communication. A working group for each was set up, and all four of these groups remain now. John Stott became Chairman of the Theology and Education Working group (later called the Theology Working Group).

As a backdrop to his preparation of Issues, John continued to make Lausanne consultations a priority. Not only was he there, but frequently in the Chair. He edited the papers from all the consultations up to Lausanne II, published in 1996 under the title: *Making Christ Known: Historic Mission Documents from The Lausanne Movement 1974-1989*. As is clear from the contributors, Lausanne had the standing (helped, no doubt by John's own presence) to draw the best evangelical thinkers globally.

The book opened with *The Lausanne Covenant* (1974) and finished with *The Manila Manifesto* (1989). Some papers such as the 1977 *Pasadena Statement on the Homogeneous Unit Principle* [ie of church growth and evangelization], and the 1980 *Evangelical Commitment to*

Simple Lifestyle gained considerable traction. Shortly before his 87th birthday, he surveyed his years in Lausanne, and looked forward with anticipation to what Cape Town 2010 would bring. He said he felt the 1978 *Willowbank Report on Gospel and Culture* merited more attention than it had been afforded.[47]

For as long as The Lausanne Movement was characterized by 'the spirit of Lausanne' John Stott sensed it was critically placed. Humility would always be needful. It is said of Lausanne that its fruit 'grows on other people's trees'. It has always acted most effectively as a catalyst. Its platform has drawn and draws from across the divides of secondary issues, incorporating the evangelical church in its widest sense – including, for example, specialized mission agencies which bring focused knowledge; Christians in the public arenas of Government, Business, Academia who shake salt and shine light; believers in nominally Christian cultures; minority Christian groups under oppressive regimes; rich and poor...

Through consultations, as leaders meet face-to-face and get to know one another as friends, John Stott sensed that Lausanne would offer a unique means for the church to share the gifts Christ gives.

Pastor-theologian

John Stott was one of the few true pastor-theologians. People mattered. We cannot strategize with integrity about world evangelization if we do not care about the people in our own town. John Stott was an integrated man. While a schoolboy at Rugby, he had founded the ABC Club as a way to provide a bath for vagrants. As a curate, he had taken boys from the poorer families in the parish for their first experience of camping. As a rector, he sometimes gave up his bed to homeless men, and slept on a camp bed in his study.

The term 'glocal' was coined in the context of globalization, hastened on by the digital world. But it describes the way John Stott had lived consistently since

'glocal' was a core value for him

the 1930s. It was a core value for him. As one of the world's most effective global public evangelists, he cared for individuals locally, whatever their status. While Lausanne would always function at a strategic level, among theological thinkers, it would be of no more worth than a resounding gong or clanging cymbal if the benefit of its networking did not touch down in real life situations.

Setting aspirations for Lausanne

John Stott's gifts as an expositor, a writer, and a thinker with wide intellectual reach were combined with a natural humility. His aspirations for the church fitted precisely with Billy Graham's aspirations for the 1974 Congress. His name had already become a byword for the diligent handling of scripture, and for a doctrine of scripture as a touchstone for all human experience and enterprise. This lent significant strength to Lausanne's standing.

he loved the chance to help people into the Pauline epistles

Invitations to speak at the 1974 Congress included some of the most able evangelical thinkers: Francis Schaeffer, Samuel Escobar, Jim Packer, Henri Blocher, the young Os Guinness, and the recent convert Malcolm Muggeridge. Stott's seminal address on the biblical basis for evangelism, opening with the dialogue on meaning between Alice-in-Wonderland and Humpty Dumpty, established itself as a classic treatment of core Christian thinking.

In Manila in 1989, he gave the first three expositions, covering Romans 1-5, on 'Eagerness to preach the gospel', 'The world's guilt' and 'Amazing Grace'. He loved the chance to help people into the Pauline epistles. Friends said that, like the Apostle Paul, he was 'obsessed by the cross'.

The Third Lausanne Congress

John Stott and Billy Graham both sent greetings to The Third Lausanne Congress: Cape Town 2010. John would have loved to be there, and briefly considered the possibility, despite his advancing frailty. He wrote:

'I shall be very sorry to miss being with you in Cape Town. But I will be with you all each day in prayer, expectation and confidence as you plan to make known the uniqueness of Jesus Christ all over the world.'[48]

no doubt there was a sense of completion as he listened to The Commitment

In March 2011 he received a copy of *The Cape Town Commitment*, and asked friends to read it to him, as his eyesight had faded. Each of the ministries and endeavours with which John Stott had been closely associated was part of The Third Lausanne Congress. All the matters in which he had yearned for evangelicals to engage were clearly laid out – not just in a document, but in a commitment, firmly rooted in God's covenantal love. He knew of the unhurried process which had taken place, before and during the Congress, to listen to the voices of evangelical leaders from across the world; to discern that the Holy Spirit is saying to the church, in terms of priorities.

John Stott had heard of plans being laid for global consultations to take forward the major areas in *The Cape Town Commitment*. It built on his huge efforts in Lausanne and Manila. No doubt there was a sense of completion as he listened to it being read to him, while sensing he would soon be with Christ.

Julia Cameron, *former board member of LICC, ELT, and Langham Partnership (UK and Ireland), has served with UCCF and IFES. She is Director of Publishing for The Lausanne Movement.*

Uncle John had a profound influence on my family. My father first met him as a teenager, when a lifetime friendship began. I remember his visits to Armonía, our ministry among poor communities in Mexico, and seeing his interest in us children learning to serve others.

I treasure the conversations we shared and what he taught me. He was an inspiration, and also a wonderfully wise, loving and witty grandfather-figure. Above all, he lived to show who Jesus was and is.

EL TÍO JUAN

El Tío Juan, con sus ojos pequeños,
llenos de inteligencia y de esperanza,
me enseñó.
Me enseñó de la disciplina,
que se nutre de ella misma.
Y de la simplicidad,
que se encuentra con la sabiduría,
caminando juntas
en obediencia;
admirando la complejidad de la Fe.

Me enseñó de Jesús,
quien es un Rey
vestido de arapos,
que camina con peces;
se sumerge en la oscuridad de nuestra indiferencia,
sangra y vuela hacia su muerte,
y regresa corriendo para decirme que todo va a estar bien.
Para siempre.

Me enseñó de la inteligencia,
que no lo intenta saber todo,
que empuja su propia vanidad
hasta no ver su reflejo.

POEMA

Me enseñó del amor a la belleza de los pobres,
a la belleza de los pájaros,
a la belleza del trabajo,
a la belleza del misterio de Dios.

Me enseñó de la asertividad,
que es clara,
ante lo turbio de la hipocresía.
Que es valiente,
ante la sutileza de la manipulación.

Me enseñó de la humildad,
que usa su corona para adornar a otros.
Que ve a los niños como maestros,
que escucha a los demás
con la devoción con la que alguien escucha a un ruiseñor.

Y se fué.
Ese señor de ojos pequeños.
Ese hijo amado de Dios.
Ese hermano amado de tantos.
Ese Tío que me veía con cara de abuelo.
Con sus manitas que le temblaban tanto,
con su espalda que le dolía tanto,
con sus bromas que traían sol entre tanta lluvia,
con sus últimas palabras de amor a mi familia,
con los últimos destellos de genialidad en sus ojos,
con su compasión y su generosidad,
con una Fe profunda como concebimos al mar.

Y lo volveremos a ver,
volveremos a platicar,
nos volveremos a reír.
Pero esta vez sin lluvia.

Eidi Cruz–Valdivieso November, 2011   *English translation* ▷

Eidi's English translation of her poem.

UNCLE JOHN

Uncle John, with his small eyes,
full of intelligence and hope,
taught me.

He taught me about discipline
that nurtures itself,
and about simplicity
that meets wisdom,
and walks together with her
in obedience
before the mystery of faith.

He taught me about Jesus,
who is a King,
dressed in rags.
Who walks with fish,
immerses himself in the darkness of our indifference,
bleeds and flies to his death,
and comes back running to tell me that everything will be fine.
Forever.

He taught me about intelligence
that doesn't try to know everything,
that pushes her own vanity away,
until its reflection can no longer be seen.

He taught me about loving the beauty of the poor,
the beauty of birds,
the beauty of work,
the beauty of the mystery of God.

▷

UNCLE JOHN

▷ He taught me about assertiveness
that is clear
as it faces the muddiness of hypocrisy.
Assertiveness that is courageous
when facing the subtle ways of manipulation.

He taught me about humility
that uses her crown to adorn others,
that sees children as teachers,
that listens to others
with the devotion with which we listen to a nightingale.

And he left.
That man of small eyes.
That beloved child of God.
That beloved brother to so many.
That Uncle who looked at me with a grandfather's face.

With his dear hands that were shaking so much,
with his back that hurt so much,
with his wittiness that brought sunshine in the midst of so much rain,
with the last words of love for my family,
with the last sparkle of genius in his eyes,
with his compassion and generosity,
with a faith as profound as the depths of the sea.

And we will see him again,
we will enjoy talking again,
we will laugh together again.
But this time there will be no rain.

Eidi Cruz-Valdivieso
November, 2011

TIMELINE OF JOHN STOTT'S LIFE AND MINISTRY

1921   Born in London on 27 April. Baptized in Marylebone Parish Church

1927–1929   King Arthur's School, Kensington

1929 –1935   Oakley Hall School

1935–1940   Rugby School

1938   Converted to Christ through the influence of schoolfriend John Bridger and Scripture Union public schools evangelist E J H Nash, known as 'Bash'

1940–1943   Trinity College, Cambridge

1943–1945   Ridley Hall, Cambridge

1945–1950   Curate, All Souls, Langham Place

1950–1975   Rector, All Souls Langham Place, then Rector Emeritus

1951   Shaped new direction of World Evangelical Fellowship

1956   Appointed Frances Whitehead as his secretary

1959–1991   Chaplain to the Queen, then Extra Chaplain to the Queen

1961   Founder, Evangelical Fellowship in the Anglican Communion

1967   Initiated National Evangelical Anglican Congress (NEAC) and Evangelical Fellowship in the Church in Wales (EFCW)

1969   Founded Langham Trust

1971   Founded Evangelical Literature Trust

1974   Lausanne Congress on World Evangelization. Chief Architect, *The Lausanne Covenant*

TIMELINE

1975	Established first London Lectures in Contemporary Christianity
1979	Vice-President, then lifelong Ambassador-at-Large, IFES
1982	Founded The London Institute for Contemporary Christianity
1983	Received Lambeth DD
1983–1997	President of Tearfund
1989	Second Lausanne Congress on World Evangelization. Chief Architect, *The Manila Manifesto*
1991	Two *Festschriften* published for 70th birthday (UK and USA)
2002	Founded Langham Partnership International
2004	Made lifelong Honorary Chairman, The Lausanne Movement
2005	Included in *TIME* magazine's list of '100 most influential people'
2006	Awarded CBE in Queen's New Year's Honours list
2006	Final international trip, to China and Hong Kong
2007	Moved into the College of St Barnabas
2008	Final trip to The Hookses
2010	*The Radical Disciple* published 'to say goodbye' to his readers
2011	*Festschrift* to mark 90th birthday *A Portrait by his Friends*
2011	Died 27 July in St Barnabas College, Lingfield, Surrey
2011	*The Times, The Independent, The Guardian, The Telegraph* carry obituaries on 29 July

TIMELINE

2011   End of July onwards. Tributes feature on the BBC, and appear in media around the world; thanksgiving services take place on all continents; photos and stories are added to the memorial website *johnstottmemorial.org*

2011   Funeral, 8 August at All Souls Church, Langham Place, London. Led by the Revd Hugh Palmer, Rector of All Souls. Caroline Bowerman, John Stott's niece, gave the family tribute

2011   Service for interment of ashes, 4 September at St James's, Dale.Led by the Revd Bill Lewis (see pp39-41)

2011   December: All papers are archived in Lambeth Palace Library, London

2012   Memorial service, 13 January in St Paul's Cathedral, London. Led by Bishop Michael Baughen, former Rector of All Souls, and 39th Bishop of Chester

FURTHER READING

THE BIRDS OUR TEACHERS by John Stott. A unique book full of spiritual lessons, stunningly illustrated. Through its pages you meet the orni-theologian personally. (Candle/Hendrickson, 1999)

JOHN STOTT: The Early Years by Timothy Dudley-Smith (IVP, 1999)

JOHN STOTT: The Making of a Leader by Timothy Dudley-Smith (IVP, 2001)

INSIDE STORY: The Life of John Stott by Roger Steer (IVP, 2009)

JOHN STOTT: A Portrait by his Friends ed Chris Wright (IVP, 2011)

JOHN STOTT: The humble leader by Julia Cameron (CFP Trailblazer, 2012)

AN 'AU REVOIR' OCCASION

'The glorious, transcendent, reality of eternal life wonderfully eases the very real sense of loss we feel, that a Christian giant, a hero, a role model, a teacher, a mentor, an irreplaceable friend we loved – has gone. This is, however, supremely an *au revoir* occasion and you do not need firsts in French and Theology from Cambridge to know what that means!'

His Honour, Judge David Turner at John Stott's funeral.

FINISHING THE RACE

I have fought the good fight, I have finished the race, I have kept the faith. Now there is in store for me the crown of righteousness, which the Lord, the righteous Judge, will award to me on that day—and not only to me, but also to all who have longed for his appearing. (2 Timothy 4:7-8)

Those who are wise will shine like the brightness of the heavens, and those who lead many to righteousness like the stars, for ever and ever. (Daniel 12:3)

John Stott with a Swinhoe Storm Petrel, on Chil Bal Island, Korea.

The Snowy Owl. This photo was the crown of a 25-year search by John Stott. Now he felt he could say the Nunc Dimittis *See* The Birds our Teachers *for the story.*

NOTES

1. 2005, April issue

2. This combined the first half of rectory with the second half of vicarage, adding a dash of humour.

3. His favourite story was 'The Lumber Room' about a boy who was punished by his aunt for claiming there was a frog in his bread-and-milk. (He had put it there himself, so he spoke with authority on the matter.) His revenge on his aunt was very sweet...

4. With Brian Draper, to mark the 25th anniversary of LICC.

5. His leadership gifts were recognized straight away by E J H Nash (more commonly known as 'Bash'), who discipled him as a young Christian, and drew him into the camps, known in shorthand as 'Iwerne', from their base in Iwerne Minster, Dorset. John Stott always maintained that the greatest spiritual influences on his life had been 'Iwerne and the CICCU'.

6. Long before that term was used, and before the phenomenal growth of the church in the 'global south' was brought to the attention Christians in the West by books like Philip Jenkins, *The Next Christendom*.

7. Galatians 3:8

8. He served as President of Scripture Union England and Wales 1965-1973. While not listing offices for each ministry, we do so for SU, as special mention must be made of it. E J H Nash of SU staff founded the Iwerne Minster camps for boys from the top public schools; it was here that John Stott cut his spiritual teeth. For insights into the ministry of Bash, who was to John, aged 17 onwards, 'a philosopher and a friend', see *A study in spiritual power* (ed John Eddison) 10 Publishing.

9. Hebrews 11:8

10. Genesis 18:19

11. Available in the *Didasko Files* series under the title *More Precious than Gold*. 'Nothing has helped me more than this,' writes John Stott at the beginning, 'to grasp the grand themes of the Bible.'

12. For example J I Packer, D J Wiseman, and G T Manley (who was Senior Wrangler at Cambridge in the year that Bertrand Russell was ranked as sixth); and later Francis Schaeffer. 'He took pleasure in nurturing the skills of new writers, would take them on walks to find out what they wanted to tackle, and then hound them to deliver the goods.' (Obituary in *The Times*, 25 May 2005.)

13. His extensive writing, of books and papers, merited its own bibliography, compiled by Timothy Dudley-Smith. (IVP, 1995)

14. It was read by Joshua Wathanga, then IFES Associate General Secretary. The Convention was named after the town in which it was located for most of its history (on the University of Illinois campus). Urbana 2003 was the final Convention held in Urbana as numbers crept above its 19,000 capacity. It moved to St Louis. These triennial gatherings, held at the end of December, have stirred a mission commitment in the lives of a quarter of a million students since they began after the Second World War.

15. In 1998, conscious of his advancing years, John Stott began work on *Evangelical Truth: A personal plea for unity*. This appeal to the evangelical church was, in his mind, possibly

his last book. It was published by IVP (UK and US) in 1999 with a distinctive design feature of his handwriting, to emphasise its urgent and personal nature. He joined us in July 1999 for the IFES World Assembly (in Seoul, Korea), as was his practice whenever he could manage to do so. We launched the book there.

16. From a tribute given by David Turner at John Stott's funeral in All Souls Church.

17. Two brief vignettes from 1959 to illustrate. That year, John Stott was missioner at two of Africa's top universities: University of Cape Town (UCT) and Witwatersrand, Jo'burg ('Wits'). Students at UCT showed unusual creativity in arranging a low-flying plane to drop leaflets to advertise the mission meetings over their steeply-terraced campus. The following week at Wits, the atheists were so incensed at the mission that they disrupted a meeting with placards and loud shouts. John invited the atheist leader to come to the front and, to everyone's surprise, handed him the microphone. There was silence in the Great Hall, all eyes on the platform. Roy Comrie recalls how the student addressed John 'as if he were an ignoramus' and challenged him to a public debate. The invitation was graciously accepted and the date set for the end of the week. The debate was crammed full, everyone attentive, as John Stott responded to each of the proposer's 17 points. The Atheist Society disbanded soon afterwards, and did not reappear in that student generation.

18. Harry Blamires *The Christian Mind* (1963); John Stott *Your Mind Matters* (1972)

19. 'The Church can render no greater service to itself, or to the cause of the gospel, than to try to recapture the universities for Christ. More potently than by any other means, change the university and you change the world.' Charles Habib Malik in his 1981 Pascal lectures, *A Christian Critique of the University*. Malik had a distinguished career in academia and in the United Nations.

20. Martyn Lloyd-Jones held office from 1947 (when IFES was constituted in Harvard) to the time of his death in 1981; first as Chairman, then as President and Vice-President.

21. From a tribute in *The Times* 8 August 2011.

22. David L Edwards, a senior Anglican, has served as Chaplain to the Speaker of the House of Commons, and as Bishop of Southwark; in 1988 he engaged John Stott in a liberal-evangelical dialogue to determine the essentials of the Christian faith. It was a model of mutual respect. Adrian Hastings, Professor of Theology at Leeds University, served in Africa and in the UK as a priest and as an academic.

23. Kingsway, 1986 p17

24. 1952. Now published by Macmillan.

25. Several friends had significant input into the vision for LICC, including Oliver Barclay, Brian Griffiths, Jim Houston and Os Guinness. Then John Stott and Andrew Kirk worked together to hone the vision. LICC opened its doors in 1982.

26. Published first in 1984 and consistently revised.

27. For example Martyn Eden (social and political issues), Ernest Lucas (science), Andrew Kirk (the Global South), Elaine Storkey (gender issues). The Institute's 'Offspring' project saw day conferences take place around the country. These led to several local 'schools of Christian studies' in UK towns and cities.

28. As brought together in *The Lausanne Covenant*.

NOTES

29. David Zac Niringyie, now Bishop of Kampala, was then IFES Regional Secretary for English- and Portuguese-speaking Africa

30. See pp 15, 16

31. See complete text in Daniel Salinas *Latin American Evangelical Theology in the 1970's*, Leiden: Brill, 2009; pp. 200-201.

32. For example Valdir Steuernagel and Ziel Machado (Brazilians), Jorge Atiencia (Ecuadorian), Darío López and Angelit Guzmán (Peruvian) and Carmen Pérez de Camargo (Mexican), to mention just a few.

33. *This is the way I read the Bible.* Contributors: Jorge Atiencia, Samuel Escobar, John Stott. *Así leo la Biblia*, Buenos Aires: Certeza Unida, 1999.

34. Edited by René Padilla (Argentina), Rosalee Velloso (Brazil) and Milton Acosta (Colombia). Published with the help of Langham Partnership, 2012.

35. Basil Meeking and John Stott, Eds. *The Evangelical-Roman Catholic dialogue on Mission 1977-1984*, Eerdmans and Paternoster, 1988. Published in Spanish the same year.

36. Stott edited a collection of these documents, and wrote a valuable introduction to it, *Making Christ Known. Historic Mission Documents from the Lausanne Movement*, Eerdmans and Paternoster, 1997.

37. My 2003 book *A Time for Mission* (The New Global Mission in the USA edition) in the Global Christian Library came as a result of much patient and systematic encouragement from John Stott and David Smith.

38. Often used as shorthand in speech and writing for The Lausanne Movement, formerly known and still registered as the Lausanne Committee for World Evangelization. It took its name from the Swiss city which hosted the 1974 International Congress on World Evangelization, out of which the Movement grew.

39. Chris Wright chaired the Theology Working Group until 2011, when he was succeeded by Dr Tim Tennent, President of Asbury Theological Seminary.

40. In 1919 we see, by contrast, the resolve of undergraduates in Cambridge to maintain the centrality of the Atonement in their definition of the gospel. This led Norman Grubb and fellow CICCU leaders to sever the CICCU's links with the nationally-respected Student Christian Movement. Their firmness led within ten years to the birth of the IVF in 1928 [now UCCF], and to the founding of IVP in 1936. This publishing house has, through the endeavours of evangelical graduates, given rise to sister publishers in over 30 nations, covering much of the world. The founding of Tyndale House, Cambridge in 1944 is another direct outcome of the 1919 resolve. Under God, we now see evangelicals teaching in university theology faculties and departments across the UK and around the world. A further part of the 1919 CICCU legacy was the forming in 1947 of IFES, now serving evangelical student ministries in over 150 nations.

41. Part I of *The Cape Town Commitment*, entitled *The Cape Town Confession of Faith*, is formed around an expression of God's covenantal love.

42. This evangelical 'breadth within boundaries' continues to be a value of Lausanne. In Part I of *The Cape Town Commitment* the boundaries are clearly defined.

43. You can listen to John Stott's presentation of The Covenant on the last full day of the

NOTES

1974 Congress at www.lausanne.org. He and his drafting team of Samuel Escobar and Hudson Armerding, assisted by J D Douglas and Leighton Ford, invited comments at each stage of the process. They received hundreds, which were all carefully considered. It was a finely-tuned and meticulous process. The *Covenant* truly reflected the mood of the Lausanne Congress as well as any single document could.

44. This exposition and commentary has been republished in the *Didasko Files* series (www.didaskofiles.com)

45. From the Foreword to the 2009 *Didasko Files* edition

46. See full story in Timothy Dudley-Smith, *John Stott: A Global ministry* Chapter 7. John Stott always maintained that evangelism be primary, and that the need to make a choice was really very rare. Blair Carlson has now been appointed in the newly-created Lausanne role of Ambassador for Proclamation Evangelism.

47. These papers are all available on www.lausanne.org

48. Then, following a reflection on Lausanne since 1974, the growth of the Church, and his particular delight that the Congress was hosted in Africa, he concluded: 'As you will be studying Ephesians together, my encouragement to you echoes the Apostle Paul. 'I urge you to live a life worthy of the calling you have received. Be completely humble and gentle; be patient, bearing with one another in love. Make every effort to keep the unity of the Spirit in the bond of peace.'

All Souls Church, designed by John Nash, was opened in 1824.

Before traffic built up, John Stott could hear clearly the 'rasping song' of the Black Redstart, perched on top of Broadcasting House (left of photo), as he served Holy Communion in the early service.

The Lausanne Movement

The Lord Jesus Christ, the eternal Son of God, gave his Church a command which he has never rescinded: 'Go and make disciples of all nations.'

'We are,' as the Apostle Paul reminds the Christians in Corinth, 'Christ's ambassadors, as though God were making his appeal through us.'

The Lausanne Movement unites evangelical leaders around the world in joyful submission to this command and calling. Our desire is to see Christians grow in their knowledge and love of God, and be better equipped to bring the presence of Christ into the professions, academia, family life and society – in all nations. Lausanne has a range of leadership networks which provide a place for theologically reflective discussion, always with the end in view of stimulating more effective evangelism.

The Movement, founded by Billy Graham, grew out of a global Congress held in Lausanne, Switzerland in 1974, from which it took its name. John Stott was the chief architect of *The Lausanne Covenant*, a major legacy of that Congress. This document is widely-regarded as one of the most influential in modern church history. A second Congress was held in Manila, Philippines (1989), where *The Manila Manifesto* reaffirmed the call of the Lausanne Covenant to 'Proclaim Christ until he comes'.

The Third Lausanne Congress on World Evangelization, held in Cape Town, South Africa (2010) gathered over 4,000 Christian leaders onsite, representing 198 countries, with GlobaLink events across the continents. *The Cape Town Commitment* (available in this series) reflects the voices of the Congress. Its Confession of Faith and Call to Action have been translated into many languages. This serious attempt to discern what the Holy Spirit is saying to the Church now will guide Lausanne's work for the coming decade.

For more information, please visit **www.lausanne.org** or email info@lausanne.org.

Also in this series

Look out for further titles in this series.

The Didasko Files (English language edition) are published in partnership with Hendrickson Publishing and may be sourced through most internet retailers. Some titles are available in formats for Visually Impaired People.

www.didaskofiles.com
www.hendrickson.com